The Townsend Lectures

The Department of Classics at Cornell University is fortunate to have at its disposal the Prescott W. Townsend Fund—established by Mr. Townsend's widow, Daphne Townsend, in 1982. Since 1985, income from the fund has been used to support the annual visit of a distinguished scholar in the field of classics. Each visiting scholar delivers a series of lectures, which, revised for book publication, are published by Cornell University Press in Cornell Studies in Classical Philology.

During the semester of their residence, Townsend lecturers effectively become members of the Cornell Department of Classics and teach a course to Cornell students as well as deliver the lectures.

The Townsend Lectures bring to Cornell University, and to Cornell University Press, scholars of international reputation who are in the forefront of current classical research and whose work represents the kind of close reading of texts that has become associated with current literary discourse, or reflects broad interdisciplinary concerns, or both.

VOLUME LIII

Horace and the Dialectic of Freedom:
Readings in "Epistles 1"
by W. R. Johnson

Horace and the Dialectic of Freedom

Readings in *Epistles 1*

W. R. Johnson

Cornell University Press

Ithaca and London

First published 1993 by Cornell University Press.

International Standard Book Number 0-8014-2868-8
Library of Congress Catalog Card Number 93-17894
Printed in the United States of America
*Librarians: Library of Congress cataloging information
appears on the last page of the book.*

♾ The paper in this book meets the minimum requirements
of the American National Standard for Information Sciences—
Permanence of Paper for Printed Library Materials, ANSI Z39.48-1984.

For Nick, Lea, and Sabina

La rosa sin porqué floresce porque floresce.

Freiheit ist immer Freiheit der Andersdenkenden.

—Rosa Luxemburg

While a soul is in prison, I am not free.

—Eugene V. Debs

Oh! There's nothing to complain about.
Buddha says: "None of the world is good."
I am fond of my hut.

—Basil Bunting

CONTENTS

PREFACE

My experience with representations of what Toni Morrison has named "white freedom" extends, roughly, from Bette Davis's *In This Our Life* to, to date, very roughly, Jonathan Kozol's *Savage Inequalities*. While it would be foolish for me to suppose that this experience, unremitting and complex as it is, has had no effect on my efforts to produce meaning from Horace's constructions, in his *Epistles 1,* of his freedoms, neither can I believe that my personal exposure to countless representations of what freedoms mean (and don't mean) has reduced my attempts to explain these poems of *Epistles 1* to a mere looking-glass exercise (one that inevitably misses the eternal and universal truths that are available to explainers who can transcend their space-times or go, in their mental spaceships, back in time). In any case, Pierre Macherey and Catherine Belsey have persuaded me, with their dissections of the interpretive fallacy, that any explanation of a literary work which fails to acknowledge its own origins and contexts (that is, some of its most crucial means of production) and its own constant danger of slipping back (the Horatian *furtim relabor* comes to mind here) into interpretation misreads itself as well as its text. What I offer here are versions of Horace's constructions of freedoms in his strangest and least (in this era anyway) talked-about book (save for the *Epodes*). If I'm sometimes impatient with other versions of that book, it's not because I don't know better. What I know is, I'm not offering here the single key to the essence of *Epistles 1*. It's merely the one I happen to have.

I'm grateful to the faculty, students, and staff of the Classics Department at Cornell for a very pleasant time while I was there with them to give the Townsend Lectures in which this book had its beginnings. I wish to express particular thanks to Phillip Mitsis and to David Mankin for their gentle criticisms and helpful advice as well as for their kindness in not carrying out the fascinating practical jokes they had designed for me as I performed my lectures. I am pleased to thank Pietro Pucci for the initial invitation to give these lectures and for the use of his office while he was away when I gave them; this dearest friend, who had introduced me to both Barthes and Svevo, knew that I would relish the ironies of that absence even as I enjoyed his presence-in-absence, for he was in fact there with me, a good, grinning "reader over my shoulder," as I struggled (there, on his ground) with the ironies of one of his favorite poets and countrymen. To Patricia and Gordon Kirkwood I offer, now as before, my deepest thanks, for their warm encouragement and their wonderful friendship. The clearest statement of aporia cannot represent how great a value I place on Sandra Siegel's generous hospitality, on her patient, always-on-target criticisms, and on her careful elucidations of what "amnesia" tends to mean today when we try to talk about freedoms. I am also grateful to Stuart Tave, Dean of Humanities, the University of Chicago, for arranging for me to have some free time in which to prepare the first drafts of the original lectures.

Finally, three special debts. I thank my teacher W. S. Anderson, both for his encouragement and help when I was beginning my Latin studies and for the superb seminar on the Roman satirists which he gave at Berkeley in the early 1960s; his Horace has always remained with me, and anything that may be worthwhile in this book will have its roots in what he tried to teach me, way back then. For the exact and *comprensivo* suggestions of

Kenneth Reckford, a reader in a million, even a thousand thanks seem small: *nam quicquid dixero minus erit*. Finally, my thanks to Marian Shotwell for her wonderful editing.

W. R. JOHNSON

Chicago, Illinois

Horace and the
Dialectic of Freedom

[I]

RUNNING ON EMPTY

> How important is emotion, indeed passion, in the epistle form,
> usually prized for its control and urbanity? How far does
> Horace's vision of serenity spring from his own uncertainty
> and anxiety? Would Horace's texts be appropriately studied in
> terms of discontinuity rather than inner harmony?
> —Frank Stack, *Pope and Horace*

Here at the outset I offer a description of what I take to be the
raw materials from which Horace shaped the interdependency of
content and form which we know as his *Epistles 1*. But before I
attempt to examine this *materia,* I want first, as a way of framing
my discussion of Horace's relationship with his father and with
his adoptive city, to look at two poems that provide useful
contrasts to the poems we'll presently be dealing with.

Epistle 2.2, a long letter to Julius Florus, to whom *E.1.3* is also
addressed, includes remarks about giving up the writing of lyric
and thus shows some resemblance to *E.1.1*, to Maecenas. Diverse as its topics are, this letter is possessed of considerable unity
of mood, that of a genial and relaxed resignation. It looks as
though Horace wants to present something like a finished product, a touched-up, formal photograph of the self who endured
the impalpable, inscrutable processes of change that are the core
of *Epistles 1*. The ups and downs, the zigs and zags, that charac-

terize those earlier letters seem to have left in their place the
serene and heart-whole person (or a plausible facsimile of him)
that Horace prayed to become at the end of *E.1.18*. At the end of
E.2.2 he is nothing if not serene (which is surprising, because
when he talked of serenity in the earlier volume of letters there
was usually a slight edge in his voice, and one sensed that serenity
was to part of his mind a better remedy than death to what was
ailing him, but only a little better). Here, however, in *E.2.2*, he is
calm, affable, chatty; he is indeed almost bland. He can still play
avunculus or shape some sharp words for the Callimachean poet
(who may well be Propertius, a poet who apparently much
enjoyed setting his teeth on edge), but very soon the poem begins
to float steadily down toward the sweet resignations of its closure. There is, of course, in the final lines—this *is* a poem by
Horace after all—just a touch of the familiar electricity, as though
he were about to renounce the renunciation and resume the old
carnality and the old vehemence. Why should he make way for
those blustering, callow youths? *tempus abire tibi est, ne potum
largius aequo / rideat et pulset lasciva decentius aetas,* "It's time for
you to turn in your chips—before the young studs laugh in your
face for being drunker than you should be, and shove you aside
as they dash off to pleasures that suit them better than they suit
you." In the *Odes,* they had, at his bidding, gone to sneer at Lydia
and Lyce (1.25 and 4.13). Were they now coming for him? One of
his amulets, one of those half dozen sacred words, saves him
from a final folly: *decentius.* His dancing days are done. It's their
time to wanton. So he exits, without a pratfall, obedient to the
wisdom he had just intoned before the crowd of beardlings
invaded, for a split second, his peace: *vivere si recte nescis, decede
peritis. / lusisti satis, edisti satis atque bibisti,* "If you don't know
how to really live your life (if you've forgotten how)—then,
make way for those who do! You've had your fun, you've had
your fill of food and drink." Then comes *tempus abire tibi est* and
so on, with its muffled memories of desire that is mocked at in
the *Odes* and its repressed envy, its near *Stimmungsbruch.*

It is a witty valediction (its touch as light as Philodemus himself could have wished it), and, despite the moment of characteristic indeterminacy (shall I, shan't I?), he is really ready to go.[1] What makes the feeling caught in this picture (the cheerful wave of the hand, the calm, unequivocal smile, in the doorway, as the darkness gathers about him) seem authentic is the very thorough and very plausible preparation we've had for it in *Epistles 1*. It is in those meditations, in the experience of meditating on imperfection, on being unfinished, unsatisfied, unready, unwilling, that we have become expert in the facets of this desire for integration, have accepted its *vraisemblance*, which we remember now and which makes this image ring true. We believe this graceful and heartening exit because we watched its executant train for it. Let me say in passing now—in the hopes that I won't feel constrained to say it again and too often (but I will)—I really have no idea whether these poems reflect (record they do not) what really happened in the life or whether the poetry "only" imagines the sort of thing that might—or perhaps should—happen in this or any life; I suppose I have a slight (and rather sentimental) preference for the first of these alternatives, but that's all it is.

So, at the end of the process of preparing to depart, an excellent departure. What was the entrance to this process? It was probably not the situation of discourse that we come upon in E.1.1, the programmatic and dedicatory letter of resignation to Maecenas. That letter does begin the process of departure formally, and it showcases the major strategies that Horace's observations on the nature of the process and its meanings will take; but what seems to me to illumine best what Horace is struggling with in *Epistles 1* and has successfully come to grips with by the time we reach E.2.2 is the ferocious self-criticism of *Satire* 2.7, where Davus, his slave, symbolizing both Horace's alter and his ideal ego, dissects the poet's character with a hatchet.

The major themes of the *Epistles* are all present in Davus's

---

[1] Rudd, 1989, 17, precisely detects the "ironic flavour for an ageing hedonist" that frames even this last portrait and puts in proper perspective its "hint of complacency."

brutal analysis. Beyond what seem the slave's central accusations, the total hypocrisy and radical instability of a man, a
moralist, a satirist, whose own life can't bear the kindest or most
casual of examinations, what interests me most is an idea that
Davus cruelly emphasizes: Horace is, in respect of his moral state
and his ability to govern the movements of his life, in worse
condition than he would be if he were his slave's *conservus*. That is
to say, he is not free:

> nempe
> tu, mihi qui imperitas, alii servis miser atque
> duceris ut nervis alienis mobile lignum.
> quisnam igitur liber?
>
> (S2.7.80–83)

As a matter of fact, you boss me around all the time, but you
fawn before a master of your own, yanked about by him like a
puppet on a string. So, chum, just who the hell is free here?

He who bids others flee their vices no more controls his own
volition than a wooden doll manipulated by unseen hands (the
image echoes and surpasses in sinister reverberations an earlier
image, at 18–20, that of a tethered animal pulling at its rope,
worse off, for its indecision, than a wretch who has ceased to
struggle against the sins that fasten it). This is a very funny poem,
and it is, moreover, possessed of a sustained violence and a
jagged momentum that are rare in Horace (not because he could
not do this sort of thing—we see here that he does it superbly—
but because the spirit that informs it tends to be alien to his
favorite masks). Why does he choose this violent mode here? He
permits, I think, a lifelong habit of rough self-criticism, one that
he usually reveals only in its softer shades, to surface very near
the end of his second collection of satires in one of its fiercest
shapes as a powerful contrast to his more affable, more flattering
masks. The design is not so much that the exceptional violence
should prove the rule of sane geniality; it is rather that an ap-

otropaic emblem of the potential madness should keep the madness at bay (and keep the sane and smiling masks honest, or at least aware of their being expendable). The favorite masks cannot say the things that need being said for these purposes. Davus can, and he does.

Self-hatred in Horace? Is that possible? Well, it is a human feeling after all, one that probably most human beings have some experience of at one time or another in the course of their lives. D. R. Shackleton Bailey's malevolent cartoon of Horace is too smug to feel this emotion perhaps, as is the bland, secularized plaster saint that Shackleton Bailey's counterparts at the other end of the spectrum tend to venerate.[2] But the Horace of the *Epistles* could feel it, I suspect, not infrequently and with a rather abnormal intensity. He was, after all, as he tells us often and as we see in any case clearly enough for ourselves, a ferocious perfectionist when it came to the making of verses. Is it strange that inside him there should be a terrifying voice—put with comic *Verschiebung* in the mouth of Davus—that told him he was a failure and a fraud? If that seems farfetched, if *S.2.7* seems only a humorous exercise in deft and gentle self-criticism (Yep folks, here I am again, warts and all, but still cute as a button), if that seems the case, look at *Epistles 1,* where the Horatian personae now say the things that Davus was saying, more calmly, it's true, less savagely than Davus had said them, but as relentlessly and at times as incisively as Davus had said them.

Goethe has a charming couplet, one of those enchanting pieces of near doggerel that a deathless amber encircles: *Dem ist schlecht in seiner Haut, / Der in seine eignen Busen schaut,* "He is uneasy in

---

[2] Neither *passim* nor page references can offer accurate guidance to the ferocious small-mindedness of Shackleton Bailey's astonishing contempt for Horace, but a brief tour of that extraordinary landscape is not without its uses: he freely voices perennial accusations against the poet that weaker spirits are wont to conceal or to disguise as praise. For suggestions about the nature of the poet's "wars with himself," see Gagliardi, 72–73; Stack, 279–80. For the venerable pastime of Flaccus bashing, see Stemplinger's sketch of its history, 35–47, 84, 86–89, 111.

his skin / Who peers within himself." We premature postmoderns are so used to the look-in-your-own-heart-and-write topos (the imperative of inwardness, the looking with a flashlight for the inner light), we are so utterly and mostly ignorantly dependent on it in its most recent Emersonian avatars, and so hostile to it as we attempt to deny our own permutations of Romanticism, that Goethe's couplet may seem to us to be nothing more than doggerel. Our own society, though it gives perfunctory homage to what went on at Walden Pond, though it makes noises of obligatory congratulation at people who make it a habit of getting away from it all (taking time, as people in the corporate world say, to smell the roses), nevertheless tends to loathe and to fear introspection. The animal that goes off from the herd is the sick animal (as this fable has it), looking usually for a sheltered place to die in. Nor is it only in modern, Western, technological societies that the practice of turning one's gaze inward is regarded with suspicion and with dread. In ancient Greek and Roman societies, too, the voluntary hermit is something uncanny, a little sinister. Cleanthes may congratulate the man who is off by himself, talking to himself (Diogenes Laertius 7.174), but Philoctetes, who has splendid reasons for wanting to be alone, is the paradigm of this figure, and he is judged harshly; the story of crazy Euripides in his cave by the sea provides another example of how convention deals with those who forget that humans are social and political animals, those who come to think of themselves as being so wicked or so superior to others that they feel driven to flee the city and feel justified in so doing. Temporary withdrawals to sacred wilderness places are permissible, but relocations there that are intended to be permanent are out of the question. Horace speaks in the *Epistles* as if he intended his removal from Rome to be permanent (and, in a way, it almost became so, almost seemed to have become so); therefore, something had to be wrong with him.

He admits this on numerous occasions in these poems. He says he is sick. If we assume that by this he means only physical illness, it is not impossible that what we will remember from the volume—something that might keep us from returning to it often—is the aura of hypochondriacal self-satisfaction that drifts vaguely through it. He whimpers a little, is close to whining; he bumbles about the landscapes of Italy, precisely as Lucretius warned him not to do, looking for a little better weather and more amusing spas. There is a touch here of the classic Ciceronian mode that may have irritated Petrarch and may well have delighted Erasmus and that Jacques Derrida has recently employed with elegant camp in his postcards: I have another cold, it rained again this morning, now it's sweltering, why do you answer my letters so seldom?—that moping, edge-of-tears tone of ink-voice. Sometimes we do emphasize such things in letters (and in the phone calls that for very many of us have replaced letters) in order to get sympathy from a distance when we are feeling put upon or out of sorts; particularly when we are traveling there may be a temptation to present ourselves as feeling poorly, to gain sympathy and so, in a slightly illogical way, to get compensation for the small, irritating contingencies our journeys tend to inflict on us. Victims of wretched weather and rude waiters and bad hotels and dangerous or unpunctual vehicles—once we have begun the sort of introspection that travel (or sickness, say, or some sudden shift in our luck or our routine) may elicit in the self alone with itself, the self begins to see itself in a slightly new way (or in radically new ways), and the uneasiness and fascination that we begin to feel at such times may well manifest themselves as something reassuringly if unpleasantly palpable—illness in the body, sleeplessness, vexations multiple and various, disorder in the outer world that mirrors yet conceals disorder in the inner world. Better small tangible evils than huge invisible monstrosities. Horace is, famously, not for an instant fooled by this most common of displacements in any of its guises (*caelum non animum mutant qui trans mare currunt,* "They shift their scenes merely, not their souls, who speed across the sea," E.12.27). His physical illnesses, if they are for the most part rather trivial, *are* real; the weather, the roads, the accommodations *are* truly dismal. But it is neither illness nor discomfort nor inconvenience that is at the core of his sufferings. They are something else. He is talking about a misease of the heart and mind, an imbalance or injustice in the soul.

I'm hardly persuaded that the bad review of *Odes 1–3* will have been a big part of the sickness in question.[3] If there were bad reviews (and there may have been, there often are), although Horace would probably not have much enjoyed being misread and misvalued by various vociferous and self-appointed arbiters of contemporary literature, that misfortune would have done little more than graze the enjoyment he took in his achievement. More likely (and more unwelcome) than unfavorable reviews of the first lyric collection would have been tepid, uncomprehending felicitations. These are not easy poems now, and they cannot have been very easy even for the poet's first audiences, who, though they spoke the language in which he wrote his lyrics, will not have had, most of them, quite the degree of knowledge he demanded of the Greek lyric conventions that he was importing and reinventing and that an appreciation of his poems (intertextuality, after all, has its pleasures as well as its duties) requires. Despite that difficulty with his audiences, there was doubtless considerable patriotic fervor in the literary world when the *carmina* appeared: a Roman had stolen one of the more prized of the Greeky genres and claimed it for the nation of Romulus and Aeneas and the Caesars. But if national pride was well pleased, the lyrics were, nevertheless, probably not much read, except by other poets. Not expecting much else, Horace would not be upset by that. The happy few, many of them the people who had seen the poems in manuscript, had done the real reading already—the rest was largely a matter of ceremony, photo opportunities, literary gossip, book chat, poetic politics (this last a special torment to him which we'll look at later). But on balance, with the lyrics in circulation, Horace was happy. What was crucial was *he* knew what he had managed to do. But it was now time to do something else.

What else but make more poems? There were *données* ferment-

---

[3] For the uncertain issue of the bad reviews, see Fraenkel, 308–9.

ing—but they needed more time. In any case, the poet wanted a rest. Why not get away from it all for a while? Why not silence the "chunes in the head" and the dazzle of images and the making of the contraptions that fuse them? Why not just do nothing? Perhaps we needn't descend into the slippery, winding tunnels of the psyche after all. Maybe the anger we find barely suppressed in *E.1.19* was fueled by temporary troubles on the literary scene. Having made a long, sustained, and successful effort to restore lyric poetry to life in a language and an era that were alien to it, he was too tired to grapple with the squabbles of Grub Street. He wanted to enjoy the warm, weary sense of his accomplishment and to diminish the anxious hollowness that follows on hard toil that issues in accomplishment. What was called for was a long, serene vacation away from writing, away from writers, away from the city.

Such sensible resolutions to the question of Horace's sickness, satisfying though they may be in some ways, go only so far; they are no better for our purpose—to close with the *donnée* of the *Epistles*—than a precise diagnosis of his physical maladies would be. They represent contributing causes, perhaps, but they do not explain away the muffled anger that appears in some of the letters (not least in those to Maecenas: 1.97ff., 7.24ff., 19.35ff.), or the occasional hints of desperation. Even if we add to these rationalizing explanations a genuine reason for this sort of disorientation, namely, that Horace had learned from writing his difficult songs what most good writers know—that writers are mostly only happy when practicing their art, when the fingers that grasp their pencils are shaping an order on the page that they can't find in the world outside them or even, until they put it there, in the world inside them—even when we have done that, we still have not accounted for all the turmoil that moves beneath the surface of these poems. As Matthew Arnold puts it in this astonishing fragment:

> Below the surface—stream, shallow and light,
> Of what we *say* we feel—below the stream,
> As light, of what we *think* we feel,—there flows

HORACE AND THE DIALECTIC OF FREEDOM

With noiseless current, strong, obscure and deep,
The central stream of what we feel indeed.

What is the "noiseless, obscure, deep current" in the *Epistles?*
Isn't it maybe composed, in what we've come to regard as the
normal way of these things, of desires frustrated and repressed,
of anger and resentment that find disguises or submerge themselves only to burst forth in slips of the tongue or compulsive
gestures? This is everyman's and everywoman's story, as Freud
taught us to listen for it. We first hear Horace's version of it (or
rather, of a portion of it) in the first volume of the *Satires,* when
he is trying on masks to find the ones that are suitable to him and
his time and place. By the time he completes the second book of
satires, the mask of the genial satirist (who rattles Shackleton
Bailey's cage so expertly) has found its perfect form. While
finishing the *Satires,* he was making, in the *Epodes,* some uncertain experiments with another sort of mask (one that sometimes
lets the rage rage on for a bit), but when he turned to composing
the *Odes,* he shaped, for the three books that would make up his
first lyric collection, a series of masks, which did not exclude that
of the genial satirist, which were as diverse as they were flawless,
and which, most important of all, compelled him, because of
their difficulty, to perfect the art of the changing of the masks, to
bring to it such dexterity and such precision that we almost
forget that this richly varied and supremely balanced poetic personality (this collage of masks) has any story of its/his own.
(Escaping the wolf and the fallen branch, throwing away the
shield, being rescued by Mercury—all the outrageous, surreal
conventions of fictive autobiography merge with vivid images of
everyday modern, or "real," life to present not so much a person
as an author, someone with the talent to collect and decorate and
wear all these masks adroitly.) So subtle is the interdependent,
mutual dissolution of fact and fiction, and so completely is the
poet fused with his genre, that he comes to seem (as we read and
reread the poems, over years, over decades) as timeless as lyric
itself, as the songs he makes for our pleasure and edification. But

here, in the *Epistles,* with something that smacks of the theatrical gesture, all the masks are suddenly put away for good and all, so the poet says. And maybe he means it, in a way. But of course he can't quite mean it (otherwise, why write? and how write?). What is the mask now? What is the new mask of?

It is in the process of being molded and fitted as the first letter, to Maecenas, begins. Here, Flaccus mimes the Enchanter Disenchanted, almost as if he had read, without great reverence, the closing scenes of *The Tempest: nunc . . . et versus et cetera ludicra pono,* "Now I put away my verselets and my other pretty toys. Too old."[4] (He is only in his early forties, but this really was an advanced time of life in those hard-for-us-to-imagine days before jogging and health food and Grecian Formula had extended our adolescence indefinitely.) He is prematurely grey, and perhaps he therefore claims prematurely to feel really elderly (*non eadem est aetas, non mens*). I'm not as young as I once was, and I've lost the vigor, the hunger, that moved my art—I'm simply not up to it anymore. Indeed, I feel rather as a gladiator must who has been

---

[4] A just sense of the spectrum of opinions about the "actuality" of the letters, their relation to the "real life," and the facticity of the philosophical commitment can be got from the following: Courbaud's faith in their interwoven realities, which seems to center on intimations of senescence as prime mover of the poems, 36–40 (it is useful to compare here Olney's remarks on the topos of trauma in autobiographical fictions, 24–25). Too old now for lust and lyrics, just old enough for Will Durant in the old folks' home: McGann, 12, 34–35, sees the prematurely senile jettisoning not merely of lyric but also of satire, "a farewell to all verse," as condign prelude to the writer's absolute dedication to what appears to be, in this view, versified and wholly earnest philosophy; he nevertheless doubts that the poems have anything to do with the life and regards all hints of psychic misease as fictions to enhance the philosophical enterprise. Williams, 28–30, 565–69, sees well enough that the letters might have as their contemporary title "How to Have Fun with Philosophy," but he doubts any important connection between the poems and the life, and he refuses to entertain the possibility that the flippancies are, in the Socratic-Cynic tradition of *to spoudogeloion,* serious. See also Macleod, 1979, 23, on Horace's "need" for philosophy. For a succinct formulation of the balance of art and life that decorum requires here, see Kenney, 229.

on display season after season (*spectandum satis*) and who is now
entitled to claim his freedom from this bloody, agonizing job
(mixing it up in the arena, mixing it up in the poetry world) and
who does in fact ask for his freedom (*et donatum rude*), which he
will spend hiding in the country (*latet abditus agro*) for fear he
should else be shanghaied back to Rome and made to resume his
deadly career. So, Maecenas, guessing that Horace is not just
taking a brief break from the making of poems, wants to lock
him up again in the old gladitorial school and thereby rescind the
well-earned and proudly claimed emancipation. What freedom is
this? Freedom from being a poet? From his patron? From his
readers? Surely this emphasis on freedom strains an analogy
(gladiator/poet) that is already somewhat too taut? Even grant-
ing that Maecenas would surely see some humor in the analogy,
there is something odd, and a little unpleasant, here: Horace is
not like the gladiator Veianus, and writing poetry is not like
being condemned to hack one's way out of the theater of death—
and, in any case, Horace was certainly already free.

Suppose that Horace, at this time, *feels* like Veianus—old;
worn out by being gawked at, in the street, at the theater, at
readings; tired of providing, with strenuous effort that must look
lighter than a breeze on a still pond, what people took to be mere
diversion; desperately in need of a permanent escape from the
slavery of being on display, of entertaining, of competing at
entertaining; bored to tears with being what Gertrude Stein
ingeniously called "a publicity saint." Suppose that even before
falling into this somewhat irrational mood, Horace had not *felt*
free—free of various obligations to Maecenas and other great
men, to other poets, to his readers, above all, perhaps, to his
own austere demands? Suppose that now, having completed the
nearly hopeless task and having given the *Odes* to the world,
suppose that, already weary and vulnerable, he was suddenly
fastened on by postpartum depression or by the anxiety of success or by the Roman version of more-than-mid-life crisis—
jargon à son goût? Or—this is crucial perhaps—by the now too
infrequent invitations of Augustus? Or by fears of impending

death? Or by all of these combined at different times and in different configurations? Or suppose that Horace sees that poetry, though it had made him happy when he was mesmerized by the task of writing it (and especially so during this last encounter), does not seem to make him happy now that he is, temporarily perhaps, but also permanently perhaps, not writing it?

Now that the joy of writing them is or seems over—for how could he go back to the *Odes,* or beyond them?—Horace can look back at the unintended consequences that becoming and being a famous poet had created. Readings and testimonies and recommendations, the purveying of poetry, the politics of poetry, the poetry world, all of which *E.*1.19 gathers into its savage light; on top of that, the politics of Augustus, who was ever more eager to fuse his politics with those of poetry. All of which was a big price to pay for having worked very hard to win the chance of becoming what in fact one was, a poet. While the poems were being written, before the grey hair arrived and the endless trickle of small, irritating illnesses and all the absurd realities of late middle age with their clear intimations of mortality, though Horace saw the price for being a poet *was* big, the price seemed right, and he was willing to pay it. But not now. Now he has other things on his mind; he has to look at his life in a different way; he has to get ready for facing the end of everything. And, finally, he has to start looking more closely at a fact that frightens him, one that he had in various ways kept hidden from himself, at the back, in the corners of his mind. He must look at what Davus in *S.*2.7 chides him for and also symbolizes: his own servitudes. He asks in the first epistle for freedom from what now seems poetic bondage, maybe in the hope that when that freedom is won or conferred, other freedoms may come with it.

Poetry had in fact made him free, made him feel free, so free in the joy and strength of creation that he could almost ignore the poetry world as he could almost ignore the worries and insecurities of the troubled reign of Augustus in the twenties. But that freedom, which he had come to believe in, to claim as if it were a birthright, had come more and more to seem less and less substantial.[5] Had he ever been free, had anyone? Yet people had always assured him that he was or was about to become free. Why had they lied to him? And why had he believed them—if he did?

His father had told him that he was free and would be more free still. And, in a way, in a different way, his teacher, old Orbilius, had promised him the same thing. Then, in graduate school, at Athens, at freedom's very source, his brain churning with thoughts of freedom that the crumbling monuments of Periclean glory evoked, Cicero's drunken son had said it: Do we dare to live as free men? That had seemed as exciting then as it seemed funny and pathetic now. Then Brutus himself had said it—and the promise of courageous and rational freedom from those austere and passionate lips sounded not only exciting but (alas) also utterly plausible. And then—

Then he had returned from the stupid war, no longer free, to a humiliating salvation and a dead-end, very dull job. And then—beyond all hope, dropped from the sky—freedom found again—in the verses. First Pollio and Messalla and Vergil said, This,

---

[5] Macleod, 1977, has very useful things to say about the relationship between art and life in Horace's art and life, and he brings freshness and imagination to his scrutiny of this Horatian obsession (see, in particular, 365, his equation of the "neglect of craft" with "moral error"). At the same time, Horace knew precisely what Yeats was singing about in the lines "The intellect of man is forced to choose / Perfection of the life, or of the work." That is to say, he knew that there are some things that the miracles of artistry can't accomplish, that there are moments when, away from his writing desk, for instance, the artist is "merely" human, no better off than his neighbor, and maybe, by virtue of the raw nerve endings that abet his craft, much less well off in the living of life. He would, in any case, have been surprised to learn that, weighed against philosophy, "the poetry does not matter" (thus Macleod summons into the debate the figure of T. S. Eliot at his most country-parson smarmy to confirm his thesis that it is the matter that matters, 363; Macleod, 1986, repeats this strange notion from the writer of *The Four Quartets* when he remarks of E.1.19 that it shows "a double vision of poetry . . . as a version of the moral life and as a mere distraction from it, or worse"; there are similar denigrations of poetry on xv, 57, 69).

being a poet, is a way for you to be truly free. Then Maecenas said it and made it stick. Free again, free at last. Freedom was apparently something you kept finding and losing. It depended perhaps on one's mood, how one saw it, how one felt about it, but, certainly, it also depended on "who's in, who's out." Now, however, in 23 or 22 (the date may be important, but we'll probably never know it for sure), Maecenas was out, after his brother-in-law's crazy, useless efforts at conspiracy. Quite apart from that, Augustus had almost died from natural causes, which would have meant chaos come again, and the jitters that fastened on everyone during that grave sickness showed precisely both how little expendable he was and how fragile and in fact how unreal all this peace and law and order really were.

So, then, what precisely was freedom? Clearly Plato was right, but, in their different ways, so were Zeno and Epicurus (and Cato, the elder no less than the younger, was wrong). What ordinary people called freedom was an illusion. In the real world (the world philosophers saw, not the worlds politicians fabricated) the truth was bondage—human bondage—to power and to necessity and, worst of all, to one's own delusions about goodness and happiness and freedom. Freedom, real freedom, would be, if it existed, something in the mind, in the soul, something laid up in heaven (where, though everyone forgot it, Socrates insisted the republic had its only place). As the Stoics and Cynics said, in their very different ways: I am a citizen of everywhere.

But the trouble with philosophers was that they were abstract and dogmatic and boring—and what they mostly really wanted was converts, was a paying, captive audience.[6] So even there,

[6] The best description of Horace's place on (or rather, off) the philosophical spectrum is Funaioli's (see Gagliardi, 64 n. 12): *epicureo di temperamento italico.* He is a rather neurotic creature, of astonishing genius, considerably more than *moyen sensuel,* who lives mostly in and for his art but who is nevertheless not uninterested in the claims of life upon him. This doesn't add up to his having become or ever having been in danger of becoming a devotee of any school; nor did the large promises and small performances (from his perspective) of philosophy make it worthwhile to make a system-

in the philosophical scrolls, where truth flickered faintly—for it was a useless, despairing sort of truth if what you wanted was to live your life—more unreality, another servitude. And the truth of poetry, his special brand of truth, the truth of making poems—what of that? Another pretty fib maybe. Neither better nor worse than the others, except that this was his own. It had worked for him and very well, but it worked for him now no more, now when he needed it most, now when death was closing in on him and all the other balms and soporifics were losing their efficacies, when time and circumstances bade him look again into an empty mirror.

Time to begin the search again. Freedom to do as one pleases (*quacumque libido est,* / *incedo solus,* "Wherever caprice takes me, there I amble alone," *S.*1.6.111–12); freedom from mistreatment and from injustice (the good *cliens, civis Romanus sum*); freedom to give to the culture, to the life of the city, what one had to give: freedom meant too many things and so ended by meaning not much of anything. So, from the fragments of the dream, slowly, slowly, piece by piece, put it together again. What does freedom mean to *me, now, here,* at this latest and not improbably last turn in the road?

What forms Horace's personal (real-life) search for the springs of his freedom may have taken outside these poems, outside the action of composing them, we can never know. The version of that search he chooses to give us is the poems themselves, the book that consists of them, and the story of the search that the poems and their book imply ("imply" because they never tell or show that story directly; their mimesis is deliberately, alluringly, fragmented and oblique). In attempting to discover what fueled that search I've decided to begin with the anger that the poems all but conceal. I do this not to follow fashion slavishly but because I

---

atic (and unfunny) commonplace book of them (that is, to become an eclectic). For a good statement of Horace's (quite rare) independence in reflecting on human experience, see Breguet, 1956, 87–89; Ooteghem, passim; Perret, 117–21; Mayer, 1986, 71–72. For a well-argued criticism of Horatian individualism, see Strodach, especially 17–19.

believe that whatever their final meanings and uses works of literature have their roots in desire, in desire thwarted, in desires whose satisfactions eluded the desirer yet left on her and him their indelible mark. Whatever functions the poem performs for its readers, for its poet its composition is a way of imagining the fulfillment of desire or of the liberation of, the freedom from, desire (by "desire" here, I mean something, of course, as trendy as Lacan but also something as antique as Plato's wonderful prose poem on the birth of Eros from the union of Poros and Penia, Contrivance and Poverty). All desires, both those that are or seem fulfilled as well as those that are or seem unfulfilled, together with whatever promises their fruition and whatever effects their disappointment, all desires—or rather all language about desire, that is to say, in a certain way, all language—are what we have come to call the unconscious. Because in the rendition of them that I'm offering the *Epistles* are very much "about" a case of apparent (and temporary) failure of artistic creation, the ability and the freedom to create, I've taken for the title of the next chapter a famous phrase from Yeats's famous poem on this crucial and distressing topic:

> These masterful images because complete
> Grew in pure mind but out of what began?
> A mound of refuse or the sweepings of a street,
> Old kettles, old bottles, and a broken can,
> Old iron, old bones, old rags, that raving slut
> Who keeps the till. Now that my ladder's gone,
> I must lie down where all the ladders start
> In the foul rag and bone shop of the heart.

Though in my final chapter I argue that these poems are as sanguine (in their dandy way) as they are clear-eyed and mature, that they give us hope for the possibility of finding and keeping some semblance of good hope about the living of our lives, I must first work through the less-than-agreeable soil in which that final faith-in-becoming grows. What nourishes these poems are suffering and fear, resentment and anger.

[2]

IN THE RAG
AND BONE SHOP

. . . one who had conveniently forgotten his father's slavery—or remembered it too well.

—Pliny, Letters 3.14.1

By LIBERTY is understood, according to the proper signification of the word, the absence of externall Impediments: which Impediments may oft take away part of mans power to do what hee would; but cannot hinder him from using the power left him, according as his judgement, and reason shall dictate to him. . . . There is written on the Turrets of the city of Luca in great characters at this day, the word LIBERTAS; yet no man can thence inferre, that a particular man has more Libertie, or Immunitie from the service of the Commonwealth there, than in Constantinople. Whether a Commonwealth be Monarchicall, or Popular, the Freedome is still the same.

—Hobbes, Leviathan (I, 14; II, 21)

In the reign of the divine Augustus men's words were not yet hazardous to them, though they could cause them difficulties.

—Seneca, De beneficiis 3.27.1

It isn't my intention in these next few pages, I hasten to say, to try transforming Horace into Rat Man, but since Horace did

have a father and since he mentions him in some of his earlier
poems with an emphasis and an affection that literary models—
Demea, for instance—or other modes of the intertextual don't
quite manage to account for, it seems to me reasonable to begin
my discussion of Horace's rag and bone shop by looking at his
versions of his father and the images they offer us of the poet's
conflicts and frustrations with regard to freedom. What I'm
taking for granted here, for the purpose of argument, is that
Nietzsche's theory of the origins and functions of human consciousness in its relations to language, as he sketches it in *The
Joyful Wisdom* (5.354), is substantially correct (or at least plausible
and intriguing).[1] His theory, as I paraphrase it, is this: as the most
endangered and otherwise helpless of animals, human beings, in
their need for one another's help to secure food, to survive long
enough to accomplish replication, and in general to get out of
harm's way, must be able to signal efficiently their wants and
needs (for example, requests for help, commands to flee or attack, news about food, whether getting it or becoming it). It is
the parental voice (in some cases Dad's; in some cases Mom's; in
some, both, if unequally) that early on crystallizes and continues
to represent as archetypal this complex system, this network, of
commands and prohibitions (some of them masked as polite
requests) which is (perhaps) born along with us, inside us, *in
potentia* when we struggle from the womb and which we also
continue to internalize, elaborate, and modify as we grow, listening to the voices (the commands) of fathers (and mothers). This
system, which includes a capacity for (later) issuing commands
as well as for listening to them, has become by the time we are
young adults so indistinguishable from our deepest sense of
ourselves, so thoroughly one with our minds and hearts, so
completely and so simultaneously outside and inside us, that it
comes to seem to (most of) us no less necessary for our survival
than the air we breathe or the water we drink or the food we eat

---

[1] Instead of "human consciousness," however, let's confine the question
to dead and living white guys, as a glance at Tannen's lucid descriptions, 40–
48 and passim, might persuade us to do.

or the sleep we sleep. This, our human speech (which, as some now think, a sentimental humanism would disguise in the specious virtues of *ratio atque oratio*) is Nietzsche's tribal language and is also, *mutatis mutandis,* something like Lacan's version of Freud's unconscious.

It is also, to my mind, what Horace focuses on when he portrays his father (*S*.1.4) giving him instances, from the people they see around them as they walk the streets of Rome, of what to avoid (and, by implication, or by process of elimination, of what to embrace). In thus instructing his son, the father had actually helped to make a satirist of him (*liberius si / dixero,* 1.4.103–4), though, on the surface of this section of the poem, Horace uses the memory of his father as cataloguer of vices to substantiate his claim that he himself is free of major character flaws (*ex hoc ego sanus ab illis,* 129). Thanks to his father's prohibitions and to his constant surveillance (118f.; *S*.1.6.82f.), Horace reached maturity without severe blemish to mind, body, or reputation and was thereby well prepared thereafter to fend for himself in life (*nabis sine cortice,* 120), and, free from vice and no longer in need of moral prescription, he is able to lead his life freely (swimming when and where he has a mind to) because he will want only what is good.

In this passage the father offers no explanation for his moral observations. Someday, he says, Horace will study with philosophers who will be able to provide him with intellectual foundations for the parental morality now handed over to him; for himself, he'll be glad if he can just stick to the ancestral ways and keep his boy safe and sound, in body and soul, as long as he needs someone to ride herd on him:

> sapiens, vitatu quidque petitu
> sit melius, causas reddet tibi: mi satis est si
> traditum ab antiquis morem servare tuamque,
> dum custodes eges, vitam famamque tueri
> incolumem possum.
> (115–19)

A small but iridescent irony for the *Epistles* is that study with the philosophers would make of his son a skeptical pluralist who ironized the word *virtus* brilliantly, not so much to dismember or deconstruct it as to burnish its myriad facets. Another, rather larger irony lurks in *traditum ab antiquis morem. mos? maiorum?* Which? Whose?

Such questions should give us pause. The speaker here is after all a freedman from Venusia. If this one-sided conversation, this running commentary on moral decline, takes place (as it seems to) in the streets of Rome, it is only because the father, anxious to secure his son's future, has brought him to Rome in order to give him the superior education that will enable him to live his life as a Roman should live it. Back home in Venusia there would always have been the provincial accent, the provincial bearing and atti-tudes, which no amount of money could have made up for. And back in Venusia, people would always remember, no matter how rich the father got, or how much he bequeathed to his son, that the father had been a slave. Here, in the great metropolis, thanks to its sheer numbers, its wealth of ethnicities, and Dad's cash flow, here they could pass for real Romans, more or less (the bright son's expensive, flawless *Romanitas* rubbing off a little, enough, on his rough diamond of an old man); here Horace, who was at least as smart as any freeborn Roman, would learn the intellectual and the social codes that would make it possible for him to use his father's money really well, that would enable him to lead a free, happy life, to become a Roman—not just in name or by the letter of the law but at the core of his heart, in the depth of his soul. And then people, here or back home, would never again be able to talk about the Venusian slave who saved up enough to buy himself out of slavery and then made a bundle and took his kid off to the city to make it big. After a while, they would seem merely another new, industrious family moving steadily up in the new, exciting, flexible world that was just crashing into existence.

Horace's father may indeed have had the phrase *mos maiorum* often on his lips, and he may have succeeded more or less in doing what he set out to do for and with his son: another good ethnic pop strolling with his boy into the Roman dream.[2] Nothing wrong in that and more power to him! But the son—the son will have sensed some of the contradictions behind the newly acquired dialect, the new clothes, and the new address. He will have retained some sense, even after he'd left Rome for Athens, that he and his father really were and really always would be outsiders and that they did not (perhaps) know very much about who their forefathers were, much less about their un-Roman *mores;* that what, in part, made it so easy for them to focus on Roman folly—some genetic code for satiric gifts aside—was that they stood outside it, looking in, scrutinizing its (for them) transparent (alien) codes from a complex perspective, one where colonial Greek, Apulian, and slavery's codes all combined to create an angle of vision that any satirist would envy. But the freedom that lucky prospect gave was not political or economic or social, and equality with real, homegrown Romans did not necessarily come with it; rather, it was the freedom of "the fool at court and at marketplace," of the court jester, who can say outrageous things precisely because he is utterly alien to what he observes and ridicules. The other freedom, equality with the Romans, equal opportunity to pursue a political career, that freedom or a reasonable facsimile of it, could be obtained (so the father thought, so he went about obtaining it) by purchasing an upper-class education for his son, by amassing the cash that the life such an education made possible would require. Which is why Horace's father could tell him—and I believe did tell him— that someday he would be free, to be a quaestor maybe, maybe even a consul and senator (I suspect that's what Dad had in mind). It is these aims that explain why Horace enjoyed the luxury of going off to graduate school in Athens (and what that could cost we know from Cicero's remarks about his son's "education" there at just the same time), to a place where he would learn for himself what philosophers have to teach about eth-

[2] See Anderson, 40.

ics and where, too, he would encounter Brutus and secure his knighthood faster than even his father's sanguine dreams had permitted him to hope was possible. But then would come the sudden end, as it first seemed, of the father's dream, and when Horace returned from the defeat of the cause of the traditional oligarchs, even after he had been pardoned for his youthful indiscretion by the founder of the new oligarchy, mere money— one guesses his father had managed to sequester a hefty chunk of it, since Horace was able to buy himself a post in the bureaucracy—could not get the old dream back on track. Horace was reduced—though it took him a while to realize that even this much was left to him—to the freedom of the fool.

The fool's freedom is of a peculiarly contingent kind because it relies on the whim or hidden agenda of those who confer it for their own pleasure or business:

> quacumque libido est,
> incedo solus, percontor quanti holus ac far,
> fallacem Circum vespertinumque pererro
> saepe Forum.
>
> (*S.*1.6.111–14)

Wherever caprice takes me, there I amble alone. I ask the price of the greens, of the flour. Often at dusk I bumble about through the sleazy Circus or through the Forum.

These lines initiate one of the most extensive of the poet's self-portraits, a collage of snapshots from an ordinary day in the young poet's life (he is here, very roughly, in his late twenties), placed near the center of his first book, in a great poem that contrasts the poet's life with the harassed and vapid lives of those whom wretched ambition devours: *domesticus otior. haec est / vita solutorum misera ambitione gravique,* (After work and a little light exercise and light lunch) "I while away my leisure hours *chez moi*—such is the life of those who are free of grievous ambition," 128–29. The neoteric watchword, *otium,* is very emphatic here in its verbal form and its final position in its sentence, and it here flaunts the supreme (and decadent) liberty: unbridled, unproductive, selfish caprice. This is to say, work (*lecto / aut scripto quod me tacitum iuvet,* 122–23) is casually, ironically trivialized as the business in the life of a dandy and *littérateur;* he strolls, unaccompanied, through the city, observing its varied and shifting scenes, contemplating things as they appear and things as they are, a sort of archaic Baudelaire, God's *flâneur,* God's spy.[3] How did he manage to obtain this privileged *otium,* this exemption from the blood, sweat, and tears that are required of the shyster and the party hack and the yes-man, or—remembering his father—of the businessman, or of most of his contemporaries, whatever their station or their profession? Sheer luck—if we view this question in a certain way—should get much of the credit for gifting him with this extraordinary leisure, but that luck first appeared (to him, to his father, if his father was still alive in 42) as monstrous misfortune that had seemed to ruin his life and all of his father's hopes and plans for him (cursed blessings, blessed curses).

Earlier in this poem, however, a poem on the dangers of ambition that ends in a celebration of the poet's freedom, another version of the story of the winning of this freedom is presented, and it is in this version that Horace's most eloquent expression of his love for his father appears. Here again the father's love was shown in his giving moral education, this time not education that he personally gave, but equally important education that he made possible:

> atqui si vitiis mediocribus ac mea paucis
> mendosa est natura . . .
>
>   .   .   .   .   .
>
>   . . . purus et insons
> ut me collaudem, si vivo carus amicis,

[3] The antinomies of the *flâneur* find definitive descriptions by the archetype's essential discoverer, Baudelaire, 9–10 (see also, less to the immediate point, 26–29). There are more differences than similarities between Baudelaire's figure and Horace, but the similarities are striking. See Breguet, 1956, 89, for Horace as *flâneur* and *paresseux.*

causa fuit pater his, qui macer pauper agello
noluit in Flavi ludum me mittere.

                    (65–66, 69–72)

> But if my character is marred with few vices and those mi-
> nor . . . if I am essentially untainted, innocent—to give myself
> a little pat on the shoulder—if I have the affection of my
> friends—all this I owe to my father. He wasn't that well-off,
> had only an acre or so. But he didn't want to send me off to
> Flavus's school.

This section of the poem begins with the luck that permitted
Horace to become relatively virtuous, and shaping that luck was
the hand of his father, who, though a modest farmer (this is
reinventing the truth hugely), could not stand to see his son
attend an inferior local school with the sons of centurions and
insisted in taking him off, personally, to Rome to an education
worthy of a knight's son or a senator's (76–78) and in outfitting
him in grand and proper style for this rich man's education in the
world's capital.

Seeing Horace in his spiffy clothes and with his slaves, one
might well have thought that all this was made possible with old
money (*avita / ex re praeberi sumptus mihi crederet illos,* 79–80). The
ideal spectator of this unusual young schoolboy might have
thought that—except for the fact that his loving father, anxious
for his son's chastity, went around with his son to his teachers
(*ipse mihi custos incorruptissimus omnis / circum doctores aderat. quid
multa?* 81–82). What more could one say indeed? The father
guarded his son's chastity, kept him free, not only from the
corruptions of the flesh but also from the least breath of scandal
(82–84). At this point the story loops back to its first intention: to
show the father's dedication to his son's moral integrity. But the
detour into what the education cost and what it meant irrespective of moral concerns should not be traversed too rapidly. The
father wants the son empowered; he gives this education, as
fathers tend to do, for a purpose. What purpose? Why make the
(fictive?) sacrifices that are hinted at (*pauper, agello*)? Why go to all

[25]

the trouble of becoming his son's *paedagogus,* performing a service for him that a loyal slave could certainly have performed for
both the son's and the father's benefit?

But let us finish the passage and then return to these questions.
Horace has been saved by his father's sedulous protection from
corruption, but, wonderful though that was, his father did more.
The language is—something rare in Horace—rather snarled:

> nec timuit, sibi ne vitio qui verteret, olim
> si praeco parvas aut, ut fuit ipse, coactor
> mercedes sequerer, neque ego essem questus. at hoc nunc
> laus illi debetur et a me gratior maior.
>
> (85–88)

It didn't bother him that somebody might someday blame it all
on him if I happened to become an auctioneer or, just like him,
end up as a broker and so miss out on the big bucks—and I
wouldn't have whined over that either. As it is, I owe him all
the more admiration and gratitude.[4]

Fair enough: the admirable father's ambition for his son and his
remarkable protectiveness are balanced by a refreshing lack of
snobbery and uncommon sense. But then:

> nil me paeniteat sanum patris huius, eoque
> non, ut magna dolo factum negat esse suo pars,
> quod non ingenuos habeat clarosque parentis,
> sic me defendam.
>
> (89–92)

As long as I'm in my right mind I could never dream of
resenting such a father. Lots of people—Jeez, it's not my fault
my pop wasn't free and famous. You won't catch me finding
excuses for myself the way they do.

---

[4] See Stenuit, 143–44, on *nec timuit;* he finds this father rather too good to
be true and is surprised by his lack of ambition. For a different view, see
Patterson, 46–47.

What a splendid *praeteritio*—one even Cicero might envy a bit! Horace has in fact spent some forty verses doing what he claims he will not do: defend his father by rationalizing the fact that he is the son of a man who was not born free and who has attained no real distinction. That rationalization, a subtle and extensive one, had, in fact, already been achieved back at 45ff.: *nunc ad me redeo libertino patre natum, / quem rodunt omnes libertinum patre natum, / nunc quia sim tibi, Maecenas convictor,* "Now I come back to myself, me with a freedman for a father, whom everyone jeers at as the one with a freedman for a father—now, because I am, Maecenas, your intimate friend." Here the verb *rodunt* and the emphatic bite of the repeated slur (in polyptoton) suggest that what we are about to hear issues from the depths. He goes on to recall to Maecenas their meeting. He had been candid with the great man (*non ego me claro natum patre,* 58; see 91, *clarosque parentis*).[5] For whatever reason, they did not then become fast friends. But eventually they did. Horace was summoned back by Maecenas, and the great world was now opened to him. *magnum hoc ego duco, / quod placui tibi, qui turpi secernis honestum, / non patre praeclaro sed vita et pectore puro,* "It's very important to me that I found favor with you, who are careful in separating the decent from the not so decent, not because I boasted a distinguished father but because you thought you saw in me someone whose life and heart were good," 62–64. It was not his lineage, then, that opened Maecenas's door to him, but his moral integrity. This, as we've seen, we soon learn was his father's best gift to him, a gift more precious (is that the jist of the detour into how expensive the

---

[5] One assumes that here he might have had at the back of his mind a parallel his earnestness suppresses: Bion's hilarious answer to Antigonus's *tis pothen eis? emoi ho pater men en apeleutheros*—"My father was a freedman" (an honest answer nobly told, then subverted by the casual effrontery) "who wiped his nose on his sleeve" (Diogenes Laertius 4.46; see the Suetonian reprise in his *Vita*). There may be more of Bion in Horace than the single allusion to him (*E*.2.2.60) suggests. See Kindstrand on Bion's connection with the Cyrenaics and his cosmopolitan rejection of poverty, 70, 77; with Peripatetic interest in individualism, 72; his own individualism, 75.

formal education was?) than a rich boy's schooling: a pure heart that money can't buy.

Let's sort through this jumble again. First, Maecenas didn't welcome Horace into his life because of the purity of his morals (doubtless Maecenas had his own moral code, but what we know of him suggests it was not one that Horace's father would have been wildly enthusiastic about). Horace became Maecenas's friend because of that enormous poetic talent for which he seems to have had a jeweler's eye (his eye for what most people, then and now, would call rectitude seems to have been, as it were, not wholly trained). Second, to repeat an earlier caveat, Horace's father was not poor. He had amassed a small fortune (not small farm) from his activities as *coactor,* enough to get a start apparently at other, even more lucrative endeavors. He had, that is, enough to transplant his son (of the rest of the family we know, curiously, nothing) to the big, expensive city, to give his son a costly education, which he planned, despite his son's unpersuasive denial, to be the first step of a long ladder that would eventually bring his brilliant son to the brilliant summit of Roman society.[6] He had been freed himself (had probably bought that freedom with money he sweated for), but he himself would always feel, in part, like a slave. His son's conquest of Rome, his son's surpassing freedom, would take some of the sting out of a resentment that could be soothed but never fully got rid of.

It can't always have been fun for the teenager from Venusia to have his dad tagging along every minute—not only did he never manage to get laid, he didn't even get to go to taverns and play dice and just hang out like his rich-kid schoolmates. And of course it was dumb to be learning a high-class Roman accent and shedding his peculiar Venusian drawl (lots of funny Greek and strange Near Eastern sounds in that Apulian dialect) while Pop

---

[6] For what being the son of a *libertinus* implied at this time, see Fabre, 209–10 (of some interest here is *AP* 384: *vitioque remotus ab omni*); see also Rudd, 1989, 50–51; Ste.-Croix, 175–76, 179, 341–42. For the kind of money in question, see Fabre, 361; for its continued usefulness after Philippi, when he bought his way into the civil service, see Armstrong, 18.

was always under foot, spouting hillbilly sentiments in hillbilly talk at the top of his lungs.

Not ashamed of his father! *libertino patre natum*. When he wrote *E.1.20*, no, not ashamed at all: *me libertino natum patre et in tenui re / maiores pennas nido extendisse loqueris, / ut quantum generi demas virtutibus addas,* "Tell everyone, little book, that, though born a freedman's son and in modest circumstances, I spread my wings, which were wider than my nest—thus adding to my genius what you have to subtract from my origins," 20–22. But by then he had almost worked through this resentment, as he had almost worked through most of the others. But when he wrote *S.1.6*, though deeply submerged, that resentment was still molten. The humiliation of the newcomer, the constant reminders of his inferiority, the unending shame from the hypocrisy of having to pretend that he (and his father) was something he was not, the sense of being alien, lower class, and second class—can all this have happened without leaving scars?

I'm not ashamed of my father = I'm proud of my father = I love my father. Horace did indeed love him, was indeed grateful to him, and undoubtedly he realized what an extraordinary man his father had been, how remarkable were his accomplishments, how powerful his character, his drive, his courage. Yet there is a dark underside to that admiring, grateful love.[7] His father had tried to use him to fulfill ambitions that his dynamic virtues, his own energies, cunning, and money, could never have hoped to close with. With Horace as his pawn—and I'm hardly claiming that he didn't also love his son fiercely and want, ferociously, his happiness and his well-being—he tried to perfect the freedom that he had won but that would nevertheless always be, at the core of his mind, somewhat unreal. The son would redeem the dreadful past by living out his father's dream: for the son *would* be free, not of his father's restrictions and prohibitions, of his cravings and his designs, but of the physical and spiritual humilia-

---

[7] In this section, I am, of course, deeply indebted to the speculations by Anderson, 40–41, on the complexity of Horace's filial feelings.

tions of slavery and of the obstacles that, after his freedom, had hindered him ruthlessly. Through his money and the education it bought, his son would be free of the stigmas that made genuine freedom for the father forever impossible.

At least some part of the son's mind must have resented being used in this fashion and in having his own freedom curtailed in the name of some vast and murky liberation that obsessed the father and would eventually show itself to be pathetic delusion. A repressive, authoritarian hunger for vindication—for revenge— dogged his every step, criticized his every movement, demand- ing perfection in everything, for only if he triumphed every time and in every way over his wellborn schoolmates could the ex- periment in rewriting personal history be said to have succeeded. In the eyes of the child, the teenager, whatever tolerable fiction fear and pity may have transformed his daily life into, this must have seemed to him something of a long nightmare, this never- ending struggle to prove one's equality in that most savagely hierarchical of worlds, proving it by demonstrating, constantly and irrefutably, one's complete superiority to everyone else. It was a brave masquerade when the lower-class boy from the hick town tried to lose his accent and ape his betters in dress, manners, carriage, and ambitions. Great expectations! But what else could it have seemed to the boy but horror when day after day he wore his pitiful disguise and found himself, at least initially, mocked by his classmates when the charade his father had invented nei- ther fooled them nor amused them. Only the puppet master believed in the efficacy of the illusion he had contrived.

Still, in a way that he had never intended and would never have approved of (I am assuming for economy of effort that he was dead by the time Horace met Maecenas), Horace did become a gentleman and did shine brightly in the brightest society, and, through the poetry, he became more nearly free than most of his contemporaries (and, whatever happened in the life, on the page, as the *Epistles* show, he became more truly free than most of us ever quite are—as free, in his way, as Erasmus, as free as Socrates or Lao-tzu, as free as Goethe or Montaigne or Simone Weil).

Because his childhood and early manhood had, for various reasons and in a variety of ways, been subjected harshly to the paradoxes of the dialectic of freedom, because in a way his entire life was spent in disentangling the snarled connotations of freedom and in continuing his father's search for freedom in a different direction, he came to try to examine the problem of what freedom was and wasn't with an urgency and an honesty that show few parallels in the Western texts I know of. Without the several educations that his father gave him (the personal, the formal, the obsessive) he might not have been prepared to search the word "freedom" for its meanings as ruthlessly as he came to search it. Yet it may be that his greatest debt to his father was that extraordinary passion and anger, the rage for freedom that was not content with a flimsy legalism—being set free—but that instead, obsessed by its need, struggled onward, looking for freedom, for a real, immutable freedom. What more precious gift is there for a father to give a son than that? Fathers are, after all (and sometimes mothers, too, or mothers instead), the keepers of the great lexicon where Desire (both Plato's and Lacan's) tries to learn to read its fate. In the volume that his father handed Horace, words for freedom and their antonyms were the crucial, desperate words, and these words would in fact define the shape of his life, that is, of his poetry.

Epistles 1 begins with a playful (and sinister) metaphor drawn from the career of the slave who performs blood sports, which the Roman poets dislike mentioning, and it ends with a playful allusion to the poet's father's legal status. This book of poems that Horace sends into the great world closes, with 1.20, by reminding that world that his father was a freedman of limited means (*in tenui re*—a little fudging of the facts here) and that he himself had overcome the handicap of lowly birth and had stormed the heights and managed to stay there (as his father demanded that he should, but he chooses to glide over this chunk of his history). For the rest, he is a pretty ordinary human being, at peace (almost, and after a long, grim struggle) with the world and his place in it.

This, essentially, constitutes his final redaction of his final mask. (*Odes* 4 and the later *Epistles,* including the closure of 2.2, will offer little in the way of any new information about the person and the poet, or the poet and his persons.) This final mask offers us the small and heartening fiction that desire may be fulfilled after all—in this case, that final freedom can be modestly if tardily achieved. But that fiction (resolution, completion, the circle closed: as Henry James puts it, "an extraordinary case of the equilibrium arrived at and assured") exists mostly for aesthetic reasons. The truth, as Yeats tells us in *Per amica silentia lunae,* is other: "The poet finds his mask in disappointment, the hero in defeat. The desire that is satisfied is not a great desire, nor has the shoulder used all its might that an unbreakable door has never strained." What *Epistles* 1 shows us is an imagination whose hunger for freedom, shaped by a father's suffering and need, is as pure as it is unappeasable and incapable of being deceived with the counterfeits of freedom. It is the hunger for freedom, not its satisfactions, that Horace celebrates.

Complex and central though Horace's father is in the spiritual imbalance that will culminate, poetically, in the *Epistles,* he shares that crucial significance with another figure who came to inherit some of his functions in the deepest places of Horace's affections. Like his father, his friend Maecenas symbolized, all but incarnated, the system of values, of reciprocities, of rewards and punishments, around which society, the public, civic world, revolves. It was Maecenas whose influence (or rather, whose salon) facilitated Horace's entrance into his poetic career and whose encouragement and love lasted past the time of his own dwindling power, down to the time when both he and his difficult, mercurial friend somehow managed to die at almost the same time. Like the father, then, Maecenas is at the heart of the private life, and, also like him, he acts as a troubling, loved, and hated mediator between the poet's private and public worlds.

Much as Horace reveres him, powerful though his conscious love for Maecenas is, the man to whom the poetry is chiefly dedicated throughout his career is nevertheless, much like the father, an object of Horace's most ambivalent emotions.

I need to emphasize here the centrality that Maecenas shares with the father in Horace's "network of obsessions" because, though I will be discussing the letters to Maecenas in some detail in the chapters that follow, I will not have much to say about the man himself. This failure to give Maecenas a section to himself arises from his curious diffusion, almost his ubiquity, throughout the corpus; he is everywhere in the poems (except the second collection of letters and the droll didactic—but it hardly implies any loss of love for him that he was excluded from those ironic, wholly public, manneristically monumental summations of "a life in art"); he is everywhere, from the beginning to the great, haunting birthday song, 4.11. Yet he is, in himself, almost nowhere in them. He is more than a mirror Horace looks into, and more, too, than an ideal reader who mediates between Horace and each of us, this I's special Thou, which we come to fuse with while reading the poems. But we cannot quite get to *him*. It is as if Horace, with a constant, reticent tact, were shielding his friend from the curious, insolent gaze of the mob (both the antique mob and us). In any case, if I pass over him, it's not because he's irrelevant, but rather because, though central, he is so pervasive as to be almost transparent. With this caveat and aporia, I turn now to the other figures, less loved than father or friend, through which Horace's conflicts in his construction of his freedom enacted themselves.

One can tell the story of that odd couple, Augustus and one of his more reluctant laudators, in various ways, but we will most likely never know much about how the most nearly true version of the tale devolved. The scraps of letters from the emperor to the poet which Suetonius quoted seduce us, both by the mere fact of their (delusive) existence and by their tantalizing almost absence, into wanting to believe that they tell us something clearly, that there is enough of them to fill in the huge gaps in the pattern

[33]

that they create and fail to create. They are obviously and hugely deceptive; we keep telling ourselves we may not, must not, submit ourselves to their enchantment—and then, each in his own way, we make them into a story that suits our particular version of this period, this poet, this ruler. We do this, against our will, because we are desperate for some truth here, any truth; we invest these pathetic shards of garbled meaning with a clarity and a certainty they absolutely fail of—because they are all we have to go on. No version of the tale founded on this rubble can be trusted. So, having gestured this gesture to the way things are, let me offer my version of the tale, the fictions of its facts.

Imagine Augustus of the thirties (when he was still Octavian) and of the twenties and teens as one of those suave dons in a glossy Hollywood flick (Verdi on the victrola, a velvet smoking jacket, a glass of port, the walls of that dusky, elegant room glimmering with expensive paintings purchased with the wages of sin). This man is not a fiend attempting to terrify an artist into submissive creativity, to order himself a paean as he might order a suit of evening clothes or a hit. He wants the poet to like him (to love him, to genuinely admire him, "for what he is"). He is puzzled that the poet doesn't seem to want to become his chum. He woos him discreetly (as he thinks), with a sweet patience. Which finally runs dry.

He makes, after his long, honorable, and futile courtship has turned sour, a last, calm, whispered offer of the sort that is never refused. The poet finally writes, on demand, some flashy, rather snotty poems. The *Carmen saeculare* is like a Victorian wedding cake decorated by Bullfinch, Hegel, and Wagner. The long letter to Augustus, E.2.1 (not, see below, the first short one, E.1.13) is a wry lecture on how to choose your image consultant if you happen to rule the known world, its subtext explaining why Horace is no more interested in taking on this job than he had been in becoming the emperor's private secretary, in listening, as a royal's friend ought and must, to the royal musings on top-ics ranging from manure to politics, from poultry breeding to poetry.[8] As for the two pindarics: book 4 of the lyric poems is devoted, as its second poem signals, to what amounts to meditations on, to theoretical experiments with, the epinician (an archaic and Greeky genre unsuited to modern times), when it isn't devoted to thoughts of sodomy, alcohol, poetic fame, military vainglory, and, of course, death.[9] By this time, however, the poet's ironies hold little interest for the don, who no longer gives a damn if the poems are heartfelt or not. He's got some of what he ended up wanting. He's got from the greatest living poet the requisite public acts of homage he wanted (screw sincerity!), and, if you don't get up too close to them, they look like the genuine article.

As for the poet's side of the story(ies): he has different feelings and different thoughts about the emperor at different times. His feelings and thoughts, of course, aren't accurate mirrors of what the emperor's projects and achievements might merit (from say, a stable, normal, rational person, one of whose chief interests lies in what the emperor is up to). The poet's chief concerns are his verse craft and the obsessions and hypersensitivities that feed it and are fed by it. The poet, therefore, sometimes misunderstands what the emperor is doing that is right, and he sometimes misunderstands what the emperor is doing that is wrong. Sometimes he understands the right and the wrong that the emperor

---

[8] Rudd, 1989, 3–11, deftly rebuts charges of sycophancy in the poem by showing how the tone of the letter is shaped by decorous ironies that will spare the emperor the embarrassment of appearing to be flattered. Shrewd as this reading is, I prefer to hear the tone as having a bit more edge to it: see Johnson, 1973, 155–57; Starr, 63–64.

[9] Putnam, 308, finds Horace's "metamorphosis" from skeptic to *laudator* astonishing (see also "remarkable," 18) and can discover no satisfactory explanation for it ("perhaps changes in Rome itself gave the impetus," 309); see also Becker, 9–10, 163–64, 240–44, 250–53; and Woodman, 138. For a different view, see Zanker, 158. The comments of Lilja, 72–74, 83–84, on Horace's emphasis on same-sex erotics have some bearing on the question of book 4's "multiplicity of meanings," its "real incompatibility between the representation of" its "project and its figuration," Macherey, 78, 191.

is doing, and sometimes he understands them only too well. Sometimes (actually, most of the time) what the emperor is doing has unintended consequences (both good and bad) that the poet understands no better than the emperor himself understands them (like most effective rulers, the emperor, from his first success to his last, is being steadily gathered into a pattern of unintended consequences and incompatible goods that he could not escape from if he wanted to). Sometimes (his mind is on his art after all when it isn't on various plentiful anxieties and the unample diversions from those anxieties), sometimes the poet is essentially indifferent to what the emperor is doing and saying or not doing and not saying; sometimes he is irritated because the ubiquitous emperor breaks his concentration with a silly remark at some dinner party or with some tiresome request. But the emperor is rather sickly, and maybe he will die. (To his contemporaries, in his early and middle career at least, he would not yet have seemed, as he tends to seem to us, who view him from the perspective of the synchronic triumph and glorious closure of his long life and very long reign, fortune's best darling and thereby all but indestructible.) This mental image of the emperor's funeral evokes in the poet feelings sometimes not unpleasant and sometimes not so pleasant (if he dies, the world will very probably go to hell again; whereas if he doesn't, very possibly it won't, for a while) and sometimes rather neutral (so what, who cares who's in, who's out?—it's the same bloody mess no matter who's got his hand on the tiller). Moreover, the emperor is, not as *patria*'s *dux* but on a personal level, something of a bore. He had complained that the poet hadn't composed a letter with him as its recipient (the emperor had read or had heard read, in manuscript, some of the first epistles and was miffed to find himself, so far, not among the happy few); so the poet constructed the droll letter to Vibius, instructing him on how to present the emperor with a thin volume (to thrust it upon his ostentatiously, even if he had asked—indeed begged—for it, would perhaps make the volume unwelcome); the letter "to" Vibius is in fact a letter (in disguise) to the emperor, one that will have to content him until the poet has time to engineer the vast and subtle ironies of the later, big letter to the emperor.[10] In return the emperor sent him a little thank-you note, with the usual bumptious, though not wholly unattractive, cordiality and the familiar sledgehammer wit.[11] But this exchange comes rather late in the game, occurs not long before the game ends with the final whispered question that is in fact a command. The irreparable damage may well have been done back in the mid-twenties when the emperor, new to the job and still feeling his way toward an effective republican-regal style, clumsily offered to make the poet his secretary.[12] The joke about Maecenas's parasite's table and the insufferable future indicative (*veniet ergo*) had pushed all the wrong buttons; the message had zoomed straight to the core of the poet's worst dread, to the buried places of his psyche where the son of the freedman feared and hated slave owners and slaves more than he hated death or vulgar manners (his money was that new) or mediocre wine or bad verse.

Now forget, for a moment, about story (denarratize the po-

[10] Good arguments against Suetonius's chronologies can be found in Clarke (among them that *carmina* of E.13.16 need not refer only to the lyrics, 158). The excess of metonymies for the poetic gift (*volumina, libelli, sarcina, chartae, clitellas,* is it big, is it small, heavy or light?) knots the irony of the gift neatly.

[11] Nepos's *interdum iocans eius verbosiores eliceret epistulas* (*Att.* 20.2) catches much of the charm of the emperor's winsome or jovial badgering (*eliceret*): trying to get someone to do what he wants, which is familiar enough in his repertoire. But the tone of the thank-you note seems a little strained (maybe even a bit pissed off?). *ogkodestatos* looks at the superlative girth (so *sextariolo* and *corpusculum,* as fat as you are short) but tosses in "bombastic" for gratuitous good measure (Arist. *Poet.* 1409b); the word may play on *ogkao-mai* (bray like a donkey—fat, swollen, loudmouthed donkey?), which harks back to the gift bearer, Vinius, a.k.a. Onysius. This cluster of meanings seems nasty where the other allusion to Horace's physique smacks more of the style of affectionate insult that friends are wont to trade: *purissimus penis* and *homuncio lepidissimus,* where shape and sexual appetite fuse in an Aristophanic cartoon: quite a witty little fellow, quite a charming little guy, a very cute dwarf—who happens to resemble what he values most, his prick.

[12] For a discussion of the date, see Rostagni, 115–16.

[37]

ems; that is, put Suetonius out of sight and mind for a bit). The poet writes of the emperor sometimes in one way, sometimes in another. He responds to the world and to its ruler and their mutual sign system in different ways at different times ("I am a shifting rivermist, not to be trusted": so Basil Bunting, that subtlest of the poet's modern readers). Carefully winnowed, these responses become parts of his poems' raw materials; that is, the images of the emperor that we see in the poem are meditated afterglows of varying observations, attitudes, impressions, in varying contexts. If there is a pattern to the poet's verses about the emperor, it probably displays little in the way of an evolution or regression or cycle in his convictions about the emperor and his empire.[13] It might rather be his usual pattern. He likes demystification.[14] He likes to play, as did his favorite, Simonides, the game of *sic et non* with the system of signs he lives in. He likes to predicate something as being grand or being vile, then likes to tinker with it, to qualify it, to modify it, to scumble it. It would be nice, it would even be really Roman, to believe in something (other than in irony) heart and soul. It would probably be swell. But it wasn't his particular (peculiar) mix (of brain and blood, flesh and spirit).

[13] An interesting, little-recalled version of a changing attitude to Augustus was constructed by Shaftesbury, who thinks he sees why Persius calls Horace *vafer* and *callidus,* contrasting Maecenas's *surge vero tandem, carnifex* with Horace's obliquities: the poet "according to his Character and Circumstances, was oblig'd to take a finer and more concealed manner, both with his Prince and with his Favorite" (1737, 1:369–70; for similar thoughts, see 3:249–50). Shaftesbury designs three stages for Horace's career, early (republican and patriot), middle (courtier), and late (recovering, returning—to independence of spirit (1900, 358–64); on this tripartite scheme, see Stack, 6–7. For an interesting similitude (sage deals with emperor), see Graham, 118–19 (the ox) and 122 (the turtle).

[14] The current state of the pro-/anti-Augustan debate could probably use a strong dose of Foulkes, in particular his discussions of Ellul's complex spectrum of the categories of propaganda, 10–13, and of how Charles Morris's theory of signs can help our reading of literary works and their relation to propaganda, 21–25. For demystification (by a writer not by a critic demystifying a writer), see his chapter "Demystifying the Witch Hunt (Arthur Miller)."

The jig is up! Time (inevitably) to renarratize: Augustus and his supporters had wanted (and given his position and his very real accomplishments it was not a strange or arrogant wish) for him to be as mythic in the realm of poetry (imperishable art, imperishable fame, the deathless, changeless art object forever busily and effectively forming young minds in all the school-rooms throughout the empire in the tried and true Arnoldian manner) as he was in the realm of current events and as he was to become (with the help of art) in the realm of world history. He had become mythic in Vergil, but those wonderful poems were (some said) rather murky. He needed more; he needed the trans-parencies and lucidities of Horace. Horace made him perhaps more palpably mythic than Vergil had been able to do, but he hadn't done it quite as Augustus and his partisans, the various signers in this system of signs, had hoped he would (again, the law of unintended consequences).[15] In Horace he becomes the hero of a cautionary tale about how power is won, about what power is and does (he becomes the sick lion in the cave who eats the mobs and becomes the mobs he eats but who will not eat the poet); about the need for order in human affairs (garbage col-lected, trains running on time) and the consequent tendency for humans to idealize force and worship it and to submit to domina-tion, that is, to yield up their freedom, to trade it for safety or for comfort. That fable clever propaganda could transform into myth, or rather, *eikonopoiia* could mythify it. That fable (our origin in the stars, this omphalos our home, the monsters *he* has destroyed for the sake of our civilization and our civilities) was

[15] For discussion of what the writers take to be Horace's capitulation and complicity, see Bernstein, 459, 464, 473–74; Little, 292, 349–50. Maybe we should think of the emperor/poet tug-of-war as ending in a draw. Rudd, 1966, 199–201, offers a memorable formulation of what calling it a draw might entail. He is not timid about defining the chasm between "inspired *vates* of the Augustan renaissance" and "the cultivated wit who shunned politics and wrote bitter-sweet lyrics on wine, friendship and death," and he gives a very persuasive sketch of an integrated human being whose "es-sence" is a knack for "controlled variety." This Horace, no less attractive than Perret's, takes in the "work as a whole," is not quite as carnal and as crazy as the one my reading produces, but is clearly Horace.

indeed nearly universal, but for someone who read history as Callimachus read it and Cavafy would read it (and as Herodotus wrote it, with an eye on anthropology and sociology, on gossip and on fashion, with an eye less fixated on assassinations and coronations, victories and maps redrawn, on memoirs of great men and official versions) what was universal could also be, from several angles, in certain ways, trivial, banal.

In *Epistles 1.* Horace was forced, forced himself, to recover the realities we are always finding and losing. What he found in the verse letters was a reality that contrasted sharply with Augustus, the current emblem of the sad, bad world of political splendor and corruption. That world of crowds and power, of kings and their mausoleums, Diogenes had sneered at and Socrates had scorned. *odi profanum vulgus et arceo,* "I loathe and I keep at a distance the impious mob." That is, to be sure, the voice of the ironic shaman of the Roman odes, but here and in other places the savagery of the word on his lips is not directed at the great unwashed alone, for Horace is not that kind of elitist. He warns away from the truth he knows all the aristocrats and middling haves as well as the low have–nots, and he shuts the door against kings as well. He keeps out any and all who cannot or will not think for themselves, who, not just now and then, not just when fear dissolves their will, trade their freedom for myths and barter truth for the illusion of salvation.

Horace's father, that inferior and outsider looking in, suffered and toiled to become part of the *populus Romanus.* The son, now apparently on the inside, felt himself more of an outsider than his freedman father had ever been. The shared metaphors on which the people founded their beliefs in the *res publica* and in themselves, the "hegemonic" codes by which they shared those metaphors with each other in order to go about the business of their *res publica,* these meant nothing to Horace until he had been able to translate them into that peculiar language, the parallel, subversive code that he shared with his own generation, his own generation of intellectuals and of poets. His ears (and theirs) were sensitive to the disintegration of the language of late republican Rome.[16] These listeners to and remakers of their own language in one of its moments of crucial transition were especially attuned to the discrepancies between what they had been taught the great words of the Roman code meant when they were children and what they heard—the garbled, fractured, double-speaking utterances—around them in the streets of Rome. And Horace, who was furthermore a satirist and whose nose for the discordant had been schooled by Epicurus and by Bion, could not long ignore what must have come to seem a constant awareness of how what people were doing conflicted, utterly, with what they were saying and of how what they were saying conflicted with what they intended to say or should having been saying. What they said was *vilius argentum est auro, virtutibus aurum,* "Silver is lower in value than gold, gold than goodness," *E.*1.52. But what they meant was *O cives, cives, quaerenda pecunia primum est— / virtus post nummos—*, "My fellow citizens—the first thing we need to do is make some money. Then we can concern ourselves with moral excellence," 53–54.

Res means thing. Reality then, in a profound sense, means real estate or (speak of metonymy!) its equivalent (as in our society real very often means little more than real estate), the equivalent thing that is produced from or turned into one's own wealth or into *res publica,* "the crowd's thing." In the schoolroom, of course, or in the lexicon, this configuration of things and feelings and words becomes *res publica* as community, the commonwealth, the common good, We the People: mutual protection and reciprocal salvation. Here, in Horace's verses and in the Roman code, money and prosperity and morality are gathered into and ordered around that most central of Roman words,

[16] See Harvey, 65, 66, for the "fractions" of the code in its transformations; see Minyard, 13–15, 26–29, 70–79. For a modern instance, see Baudrillard, 1988, 14–21.

virtus. But the truth of the matter is what lurks behind the lapidary pragmatism of *virtus post nummos.* Virtue after money: once you are a little ahead of the game you can begin to start worrying about ethics; before that anything done for the *sake* of money but in the *name* of virtue is as excusable as it is patriotic.

Poets and Cynics know better, and so do children. A few lines after *post nummos* comes the shrill singsong of little boys at play: *rex eris si recte facies,* "You will be the king if you do the right thing." It is virtue that confers nobility and rule (that is, self-rule, independence). All else is delusion, as children know (their *puerorum nenia* tells us they do) until they grow up and forget what they sang in the streets, as had children before them (*et maribus Curiis et decantata Camillis,* "a jingle repeated by the men of old, when they were kids, like Curius and Camillus and their progeny," 64). Those ancestors did not forget the truth when they became adults. Now the jingle goes *rem facias, rem / si possis recte, si non, quocumque modo, rem,* "Make money, money, justly if you can, / If you can't make it justly, make it any way you can, / Money!" 65–66. Rather, says Horace, stick with the old nursery rhyme: Do what's right, stand tall on your own two feet, a free man can stare Fortune down, unflinching (68–69).

That sounds a trifle Stoic, perhaps, but it's also the voice of the old Roman code—and in a way of Epicurus and of Diogenes (and all these voices, after all, pattern themselves to some degree on Socrates). But the person who actually hears, who actually *listens to,* these words behind the words of the street boys' song— where does that person fit in, in modern Rome? He doesn't. *quodsi me populus Romanus forte roget cur / non ut porticibus, sic iudiciis fruar isdem / nec sequar aut fugiam quae diligit ipse vel odit,* "So, if the Roman people should happen to ask me why I share the same colonnades with them but not the same opinions, why I don't ape them in their likes and dislikes—," 70–72; if they should ask him why he wasn't really one of them, he'd give them the same answer that the shrewd fox in the story gave to the sick lion: *quia me vestigia terrent, / omnia te adversum spectantia, nulla retrorsum,* "Because those footprints scare the hell out of me—all

[42]

of them lead in your direction, none of them circles back away from you," 75. You are, says Horace to the crowd, a beast of many heads (*belua multorum es capitum*, 76). What should I follow? Whom should I follow? I live in the same physical space as the Roman people, but in terms of what I want and value I might just as well live on another planet. I can't follow them in their loves and hates, and if one of them should ask me why, I'd have to tell him what the fox said to the allegedly indisposed lion: I don't want to follow, I don't want to join. I don't want to nourish the beast with the thousand heads.

Whether the beast is Augustus or his crowds or a conflation of them is uncertain.[17] What matters in this passage is the fear Horace feels from the threat to his independence and to his resolution to stay free. This sliver of a fable, the more powerful for its being so compressed, recalls other places in the *Epistles* where identity and freedom are lost, where the creature to whom the promise of false safety or false happiness or false freedom is made finds itself betrayed, comes to the edge of destruction, or is in fact destroyed.

So in *E*.7.32–33, where another fox, not so wary as the lion's interlocutor in *E*.1, having squeezed his way into a corn bin and eaten too much, is given unsympathetic advice by a weasel as to how to solve the problem of egress that his new amplitude has created: *si vis effugere istuc / macra cavum repetis artum, quem macra subisti;* "If you want to get out of there, try that chink again when you are thin—you were thin when you entered." Becoming what you're not, trying to seem what you're not, trading a genuine identity for one more glittering and infinitely more fragile than the one that's yours—that's the way to the loss of freedom and of self. Volteius Mena in *E*. 7 is not Horace, nor is Maecenas Phillipus, but the tale of the ordinary working stiff who changes his frugal yet autonomous way of life for one more sumptuous and less free is hardly out of place in a poem in which Horace examines the possibility of giving up, of giving back, the

---

[17] See Shaftesbury, 1900, 364.

support his poetic career has needed and enjoyed. If, like the fat little fox and like Volteius Mena and like the country mouse of *S*.2.6 and like the horse of *E*.10.35 that helps humans exploit the world, if he finds that he has jeopardized his real happiness and real freedom by exchanging authentic *parva* for unreal yet fatal *magna*—I give it all back (*hac ego si compellor imagine, cuncta resigno, E*.7.34).[18] I give it all back the minute (whenever, if ever) I see that the tale of the greedy fox points to me.[19] It's the fox

[18] "There is one form of the expression of protest, associated particularly (though not solely) with slaves, which deserves to be singled out: the fable"; thus Ste.-Croix, 444, in an excellent discussion of Phaedrus as he gets ready for the closure of his chapter "The Class Struggle on the Ideological Plane" (see also 643 n.11). The parenthesis perhaps includes Horace, but Horace, not mentioned in this context by Ste.-Croix, embraces both the fable of protest and (through his father's anxieties) slavery: these are fables about the loss of freedom, about becoming enslaved, and their prominence in the work and in the *Epistles* ought not to be explained away or ignored. It is a central image, a central concern, an obsession (perhaps particularly in the *Epistles*). Highet, 278, takes note of the obsession ("always painfully aware of the fact that his father had been a slave—which meant that he might have been a slave himself") but finds that the "queer effect it had on his poetry" was essentially unfortunate. He could identify with slaves "indirectly" "sometimes," but the fact of slavery in his father's life and therefore, irremediably, in his own made "him speak of them and to them coldly, sometimes brutally"; he has nothing of Juvenal's "kindly feeling." This is well observed, but *non solum quod videas sed quemadmodum refert*. The guilt of the survivor might be taken into account here. Shaftesbury's "dares tell his mind only in fables," 1900, 361, gets us much closer to the anxiety, the repressed horror (of being a slave, having a father who was a slave).

[19] For this, see Courbaud, 298–301. Kilpatrick, 12, translates *cuncta resigno* as "I refute it all," which keeps the tone of the letter, at least in this section of it, unambiguously friendly, but, in addition to being rather strained in its idiom, it ill accords with the rest of the letter. In a not dissimilar move, McGann, 95–96, reads the phrase and the letter it is in as hypothetical; it "has no more connection with a real world of plans and intentions than" the word *transfuga*, which is also addressed to Maecenas in *C*.3.16.23. But in addition to *transfuga* one also finds *fugitiva* in *E*.10.10 and the extended image at the opening of *E*.2.2.1–25, especially *semel hic cessavit*, 14 (this mirrors the opening of *E*.1, with its gladiator wanting freedom, which mirrors in turn the boybook that wants its freedom in 1.20). *cuncta resigno* and its letter merely enact, as McGann interprets them, what

who's to blame for his overeating and his consequent loss of the ability to escape from the place of excess which tempted him to engineer his own ruin; the fault doesn't rest with the bin he crawled into or the grain it held. He doesn't say, "Since this is what's happened to me, since I've been spoiled by the luxury *you* heaped upon me, I throw it back in your face." What he means is "If ever I discover that I am (without your having planned it that way) enslaved by your gifts, I will drop them instantly and run like hell." Similarly, in his reworking of the *Bacchae* at the end of *E.*1.16, the mention of suicide is not an idle or hysterical threat, screamed in a moment of panic and sudden realization that enslavement has begun; it is a reasoned alternative to the possibility of enslavement:

> qui melior servo, qui liberior sit avarus,
> in triviis fixum cum se demittit ob assem,
> non video. nam qui cupiet, metuet quoque, porro,
> qui metuens vivet, liber mihi non erit umquam.
>
> (*E.*16.63–66)

I can't see how the miser is any better off or any freer than a slave, I mean some guy who strains his back bending over into the gutter where kids have glued a penny. As long as he doesn't have something he really wants bad, he's going to be scared he may end up not getting it. So he spends his whole life in a panic attack. In my book that poor bastard is very definitely no free man.

---

might happen and what might be said "when an aging dependant is drawn from the side of his great friend and seeks peace in the countryside." If pure fictive philosophy (as if) is what fits the bill, why mention the farm (which by now has taken on all the splendor that the fact of fiction can give it), why mention Maecenas? Why not invent, as a philosopher might, some other farm, some other great man, some other geriatric dependent? Maybe because Horace is a poet, not a philosopher (of any kind, in any degree). For a different view, though he does not treat of the *Epistles*, see Zetzel's "paradigm of the displaced patron," 96 and 100; there is a similar emphasis in Santirocco, 154, 166, 241, again without much concern for the *Epistles*.

Such a person, whatever his legal status, has the mentality of a slave (*serviet utiliter,* 70); though born free and of free ancestors, he is one of the drones of the hive. He will slave away efficiently because he thinks that his exertions will yield him still greater security than he already has, and he thinks too that the more money he gets, the more freedom (and safety) he can buy, but what he earns is anxiety for what he may not get and for what he may lose.

But to the king of the hive the good and wise man will dare to say (*vir bonus et sapiens audebit dicere*), "Pentheus, ruler of Thebes, what humiliation have you in mind for me to suffer?" (*Pentheu, / rector Thebarum, quid me perferre patique / indignum coges?* 73–75). "I'll take away your worldly goods." "Fine! Take away my cattle, my property, my couches, and my silver. Cart off the whole shebang." "I'll put you in handcuffs and leg irons and hand you over to a sadistic warden." "The god himself will set me free the moment I want my freedom" (*deus ipse, simul atque volam, me solvet*). "I gather he means" (*opinor / hoc sentit,* 78–79), says Horace, "I'll die" (*morior*). Death is the goalpost (*mors ultima linea rerum est*). If I should ever lose all hope of the barest amount of freedom I need, I would want to die, I would kill myself.[20]

The fat fox has eaten his way into captivity and awaits death. His sly counterpart is not seduced by the beguiling threshold that leads from the imperfections of the present to their dazzling transformations in a clouded future. Horace resembles, so far, or hints he does, the wiser fox. It is the crowds and their puppet king who always crave—and cannot get—freedom (the freedom to do as they please, to be without anxiety for a future they need to control and cannot); and it is always they who end in servitude to one another and to their fantasies of omnipotence, betrayed, tricked by the promise of more and bigger and better into aban-

---

[20] Again Kilpatrick, 101, softens (or rather, uproots) the vehemence, this time of *morior,* which he translates as "I shall die," that is, in obedience to my destiny, a good Stoic.

doning the small, the authentic, the actual freedom they could have.

But though he eluded Augustus, Horace has in fact made the mistake that recurs in these fables of creatures who end by saying, like Volteius Mena (*E.*7.96), *obsecro et obtestor, vitae me redde priori!* which is a statement, a cry, a confession that might well, on one level, stand as a motto for the book as whole: "I beg you, I plead with you, give me back—give me back to the life I lived before!" By walking through the doors Maecenas had opened for him, by becoming a poet and living a literary life, Horace had in fact become part of the hive, ironic outsider though he claimed to be and was and continued to be. He had accepted responsibilities to his adopted community along with the privileges that it conferred on him. Why, then, should he complain of those responsibilities? How dare he complain of them?

Maybe he has no right to complain of them—yet complain he must. For his situation *was* paradoxical and intolerable. On the one hand, being in and of the hive, it was his function to tell his fellows what truths he saw about them and the hive. That was his task, one he was born for and one that he freely accepted. The glories and miseries that came with this territory were his to enjoy and to endure. On the other hand, he was not exactly of the hive; he was only in it, and he was also, inevitably, outside it. Otherwise, he could not have seen and continued to see the city and its citizens as they were and thus perform his essential function both for truth's sake and for their real well-being. It's not for nothing that the figure of Orpheus, long before the Romantics got hold of him and reshaped him to suit their own special versions of alienation from technological societies, was the enchanted outsider, the shaman who mediated between humans and their inscrutable powers of nature which both sustained and threatened them and their culture. The shaman must be able to tell the truth about the hive; he cannot offer to the king and the swarms only the good news they want to hear.

For the hive to function, of course, for the king and his swarms to maintain the morale that permits them to win safety and prosperity for the hive, there must be occasional compromises with the ideal, there must be a margin left for contingencies and unintended consequences and other suprarational actualities. Errors must often be overlooked, and not infrequently the truth must be shaved and angled. Reality is, after all, humanly speaking, a patchwork of such accommodations. But if the reformulations occasioned by contingencies, if accommodations of truth become too numerous and too extreme, if the discrepancy between substance and shadow becomes too grotesque, if the shaman is called upon—once too often—to sing a lovely lie (whether Platonic or Nietzschean or Pentagonian), what then? The shaman may be damned if he does; he will certainly be damned if he doesn't. The hive exists by virtue of its ideas of order, and these must be made palpable through art or some ersatz art if the common patterns and values, the shared metaphors that unite us into our societies, are to be shared and lived. The shaman must body them forth, must incant them into visibility.

Vergil had performed this task, hadn't he? (Yes, in an agony of reluctance, with a ruining magnificence, trying to ward off despair, he had almost done it, had died trying to do it.) With Vergil gone, why shouldn't Horace, the obvious replacement, take over that function, sing the hive to confidence and courage? Why didn't he? Perhaps because he saw too much of things as they were. Before his father had dragged him off from Venusia to Rome—to misery, and then to greatness—as a boy he had very likely, in addition to Latin, heard and spoken Greek and what we might have called, before Edward Said taught us not to, the babble of foreign tongues, one of which may have been his native one. If in school, even before leaving Venusia, he learned the stories of the seven hills and the seven kings, he was to see them through eyes that were not truly Roman because he heard them with ears that were not those of a native. So it is not unlikely that he was, after the elements of the language and its codes had become quite familiar to him, especially sensitive to certain kinds of nuances in the great Roman words he heard, nor need we suppose that his sense of Roman history, of its continuities and traditions and inconsistencies, was wholly colored by jingoism and other forms of sentimentality (the convert, it's true, is ordinarily fanatically orthodox, but Horace was hardly ordinary, and his conversion was never quite solemnized).

One word that he heard very clearly was, again, that central word, *virtus*. Manhood, virility, toughness, courage, guts—these are among the various facets of the word that different angles of discourse emphasize, but add all of them up and you get something like this: the physical, emotional, and intellectual force of the free (Roman) male, who is, except when his country calls, his own man; someone who can take care of himself, someone you can depend on, someone you'd rather have on your side than not, someone you wouldn't want for your worst enemy. When Lucilius discusses the word in that celebrated fragment, we sense that by the mid–second century B.C. it is already slipping into the profound ambiguity that will mark its fortunes in the Romance languages and in English as long as people continued to talk of virtue. On the one hand, a genteel, Platonically tinged meaning, moral excellence, which may or may not have physical power to back it up, but probably doesn't and shouldn't; and on the other, balls, to use the most exact of current near equivalents, which means physical fearlessness, a readiness for self-sacrifice for the welfare of the tribe, and an unalterable will to resist any effort to constrain it to betray the best interests and the values of the tribe (this version of virtue tends to have physical power to back it up but finally could do without it; it is only in beer commercials and other adolescent fantasies that macho brute strength seems of the essence for this version of courage).

But a superb definition of virtue, unlike Lucilius's complex, elaborate series of predications, never mentions the word itself. Here, from the opening paragraph of Cato's book on farming, is his sketch of the core of Roman morality:

et virum bonum quom laudabant, ita laudabant, bonum agri-
colam bonumque colonum. amplissime laudari existimabatur
qui ita laudabatur. mercatorem autem strenuum studiosumque
rei quaerendae existimo, verum, ut supra dixi, periculosum and
calamitosum. at ex agricolis et viri fortissimi et milites stren-
uissimi gignuntur, maximeque pius quaestus stabilissimusque
consequitur minimeque invidiosus, minimeque male cogi-
tantes sunt qui in eo studio occupati sunt.

And when they wanted to praise a good man, they did it in this
fashion: he's a good tiller of the soil, he's a good farmer. They
thought that anyone thus praised had been praised lavishly
enough. Now the merchant, though he may be zealous in his
pursuit of profit, is always courting danger, always putting
himself in harm's way. Farmers, on the other hand, who sire the
bravest soldiers and the toughest, get their living by toil that is
as honorable as it is secure, and they cause the least resentment
in others and are themselves least resentful of others.

Previous to this Cato has just stated that there are only three
ways for a Roman to make a living: as merchant, as usurer, as
farmer. Of these, only the last of the three really passes muster.
Being a merchant is almost morally sound, but it is physically
dangerous and therefore appeals to a taste for adventure and a
lack of prudence that verge on the irresponsible. Banking would
be a reasonable enough way of getting one's bread if it were
morally respectable, but, as the severe penalties instituted by the
maiores make clear, it isn't. If it were—the irony is as stunning as
it is heavy—the penalty for thievery would not be twice as light
as it is for making money (taking money) by lending it out. So, a
good man is a good farmer, and a good farmer is a good man.
Q.E.D. The citizen-farmer, then, can be trusted in a group; that
is, you can put your life in his hands (and he in yours) if necessary, because he is ready always to fight for *his* family, *his* home,
and *his farm*. He has a genuine and—for a Roman—a genuinely
spiritual stake in who wins and who loses (sacred because his

[50]

farm and family are sacred, are centered on and encircled by
gods). So, he really will fight to win, to the death. He will go
down swinging; you can count on him as utterly as you can, and
must, count on yourself. In short, the citizen-farmer, who instantly lays down his plough and takes up his sword and shield
when the republic bids him to do so, is fighting for his freedom
(and his property) and for your freedom (and property) as well.
(His freedom, of course, is interdependent with, identical with,
his property; in a sense, his property produces his freedom,
which in turns defends the property that creates it. And his
freedom is also interdependent with yours.)

This antique *virtus* of the ancestors, in which morality and
utility fuse in a rural innocence, in which right and wrong are
as clear as sunlight on a summer field, is, precisely, antique. It
was the object of nostalgic feeling even when Cato captured it
forever, with a suitably laconic eloquence, in that crazy and
wonderful book on farming, and it remains a venerable relic of a
long-vanished and never quite real past, a pastoral (that is, agri-
cultural) ideal, a pastoral rationalizing of empire (those farmers
forced to defend their farms) even at the moment when Horace
subjects it to the steady scrutinies of words and things that help
inform the *Epistles*. While the queen spun her wool in the marble
halls and the king contrived to look as rural as possible as often
as possible (but this was not hypocrisy, because, deep down,
Augustus wanted to be rural even if Livia didn't), the city of
Rome was finishing the process of becoming a polyglot cosmopolis where the great-grandchildren of Cato's *agricolae* rubbed
shoulders with the ever-expanding, ever more ethnically diverse
crowds who were becoming the new Romans of a new Rome—
new Romans to whom *virtus* was, as Horace puts it twice in the
Epistles, nothing but a word (*virtutem verba putas et / lucum ligna,*
6.31–32; *aut virtus nomen inane est,* 17.41). It was a resonant word,
and for all the intensities of its disintegrations and reformulations, it remained a powerful one; but, in Horace's time, it meant
nothing like what it meant when Cato, recovering its original
force, gave it such splendid form, both in the passage I've quoted

and throughout his writings. In Cato and for his ideal citizen-farmers, it meant the capacity to resist orders that were unlawful and the capacity to force others to obey one's own (just) will; it meant the freedom from the coercion of others and the freedom to coerce others (if need be) to help defend one's own property and the republic's. (And it came to mean, when the republic began to rot past remedy, the freedom to increase one's property by stealing what one had been forced to undertake the protection and civilization of.)

I'm not sure that this word ever really meant what its speakers of archaic Latin claimed it meant (or what Vergil's anachronistic, ironic recreations of it mean, as in, for example, Aeneas's speech to his son in *Aeneid* 12), but we can certainly hear the power of the ideal it gestures to when we read it in Cato (or even when we hear it, muffled and broken, on the lips of Aeneas).[21] By the time Octavian became Augustus and Horace recalled the figure of Cato in the Roman odes, and not least at their very close, in order to emphasize ironically the transformation of Rome from innocent agrarian paradise to cosmic empire, there were other kinds of liberty, and there were other kinds of moral excellence coming into being, but the peculiar constellation of courage, freedom, power, and integrity that Cato's version of *virtus* crystallizes had passed away with the institutions, with the social, economic, and political patterns, that had given rise to it.

The outsider hears the word, walks the streets of Rome, compares what he hears with what he sees, and he discovers that the word means something, means some things, whose outlines have not yet become clear, something that neither Sallust's ele-

---

[21] See Johnson, 1986, 98–99; for Horatian *virtus,* see Sarsila, 111–16, 135, who sees it as *duplex,* as embracing both an active (or extraverted) and a negative (or introverted, inwardly looking) aspect of the quality, whereas the other Augustan poets (Vergil overwhelmingly so), in the footsteps of Catullus and Lucretius, tend to opt for the negative aspect: an interesting and useful study, but the ironies that attend Horace's handling of the word, especially in the *Epistles,* are ignored. There is a good discussion of Horace and *virtus* in Hirt, 233–35.

gant echoes of Cato nor Cicero's dazzling and desperate Platonizations of the word have closed with. Horace has begun to see that *virtus* and the freedom that it tokens no longer exist, and he has begun to wonder if they were ever, in Rome, or in their Greek versions, anything more than, anything other than, hopes, wishes, aspirations, ideals, dreams. He has begun to wonder what happens when human beings realize that they are never truly free, that the varieties of freedom seldom seem to mesh very well together, that the human condition and the facts of political behavior seem to preclude anything resembling the kind of freedom that Cato praises or that Demosthenes and Cicero exhort us to defend to the death (*cuncta resigno, moriar*).

He has begun to sense, both from what he sees outside himself and from what he feels inside himself, that freedom, like happiness, is not so much a state of mind or of existing or a possession or thing as it is an action, a movement of the mind and soul wherein choices and values become manifest both in what we do and what we do not do, in what we want to reject and what we want to embrace. Such freedom, freedom as a creative process in which we design our values and live them, is beyond what the *res publica* with the technical answers to technical questions can hope to provide or to nourish.[22] Zeno and Plato, Aristotle and Epicurus, had offered versions of the freedom he felt himself in need of and which Augustus, despite his claims, could not give. But for reasons he would gradually come to fathom, their versions, suggestive though they were, could not suffice for him. Having discovered that the freedom his father gave him was not quite real and that, having exiled himself from the hive and its unreal freedoms, he was still not free, he began to guess that the recognition of bondage was the beginning of wisdom and of freedom.

---

[22] For an illuminating discussion of Ellul's "technic," see Lovekin, 152–276.

[3]

INCOMPATIBLE GOODS

Someone once said to me that he felt immense gladness and confidence on coming out of confession; another maintained that he left the confessional box still in dread. My thought about this: maybe one good man could be made by joining these two together since each lacked what the other had. We often chance on the same oddity in other matters.

—Pascal

Just after publishing *Odes 1–3,* Horace may have felt free at last (again) from his father's commands, because, by achieving so complex and difficult a design, he had in effect satisfied those commands and in so doing found that what his father valued was—at least for him—insufficient, needed to be transcended. He may also have felt free, at least temporarily, from the crowds and their king, because he had effected an "internal retreat" to a sort of internal emigration, by going off to that now-famous Sabine farm (the physical one *and* the one of the mind). But, paradoxically, he may also have felt no less enslaved than he had felt before. Hence the readings (whether real or fictive or both), now systematic, now desultory, in the philosophers (the tedious no less than the lively ones), in Homer (that bible of the great hedonists of Lesbos, his special mentors, and of all of Greece in its prime, now miserably allegorized by Stoic pedants); hence, too, the inklings of a new group of poems that would examine these new feelings; and hence, finally, the poems to Maecenas which spell out his new discontents with being a poet (such is the displacement, which is perhaps a tender joke at Vergil's expense—for Vergil had "really" abandoned poetry for philosophy), and which may come close to expressing genuine regret for having allowed himself to become a poet on the world's terms. *Cuncta resigno* and its poem (I'll give it all back if I find that your generosity is destroying me) is only the tip of the iceberg. We hear the real unreasoning anxiety and anger in 1.1 and 1.19.

At the end of the latter poem, accused of being arrogant and even of having perhaps won his poetic supremacy through his friendship with men in high places (43ff. = S.2.6.47ff.), he has recourse, in trying to describe his feelings, to a gladiatorial image (an echo of the one in 1.1: Veianus going into the country to a rural retirement from murders that amused the masses). He equates arguing, having to argue, with the freaks of the poetry world, with being in a gladiatorial fight: *displicet iste locus, clamo et diludia posco. / ludus enim genuit trepidum certamen et iram, / ira truces inimicitias et funebre bellum,* " 'That position's unfair!' I shout, and I ask for time out. For sports tend to give rise to heated strife and anger, and anger in turn brings savage feuds and wars to the death," 47–49. In 1.1 the tone is less violent than it is at the end of 1.19, but it is hardly less desperate. In complaining that Maecenas is apparently not taking him seriously when he says that he must stop writing poetry and must find a cure for what ails him (once, that is, he has been able to find out, if he can find out, what ails him), in insisting that Maecenas be patient with him, Horace somewhat bitterly reminds his friend that he worries if Horace gets a bad haircut or is seen wearing a tunic that is not quite fresh or a toga that hangs badly.

> quid mea cum pugnat sententia secum,
> quod petit spernit, repetit quod nuper omisit,
> aestuat et vitae disconvenit ordine toto,
> diruit, aedificat, mutat quadrata rotundis?
> (97–100)

What if my brain battles with itself, shuns what it's been looking for, goes back to hunting what it's just got rid of, sways this
way and that, makes havoc of what order I have in my life, first
smashing it to pieces, then pasting it together again—always
trying to do, precisely, what can't be done—would you call
that neurotic?

Maecenas thinks all this insanity *normal,* or perhaps he finds it
more or less amusing, finds in this disequilibrium signs of the
artistic temperament. He doesn't think Horace needs a shrink or
a keeper. He thinks he needs to find a better manicurist.

Maecenas perhaps can't believe his ears. This talk of sickness,
of human bondage, from the author of the *Satires* and the *Odes?*
This from the man who told Augustus where to peddle his
papers? What Maecenas can't, perhaps, understand, what the
tone of 1.1 suggests that he doesn't understand, is that Horace
has begun to see that perhaps he must practice, try to practice,
what he preaches. Or that he must at least begin trying to lessen
the disparity between what the poetry has been saying superbly
and what the life has been living on and from.

The central text for what Horace preaches is, as I see it, *fuge
magna* (E.10.32), which occurs right at the center of the *Epistles.*
But since that topos is so ubiquitous (in Horace and in ancient
Greek and Latin writing), since that *platitude* is so distinctively
stamped with Horace's exquisite styles of discovering variations
for it as to be almost meaningless in respect of its content,
perhaps we should first examine it in a much earlier, and rawer,
formulation: *phileein gar ek tōn malakōn xōrōn malakous genesthai,*
"Soft countries tend to produce men that are soft." Is that final
page of Herodotus also platitudinously transparent? One has the
impression sometimes in reading descriptions of Herodotus that
Cyrus's witty, terrifying pronouncement either is not being no-
ticed or is being ignored (as if it were not there or were better not
there). Maybe it seems too similar to other old saws that warn
against an optimism born of and dependent on triumph or wind-
fall: power tends to corrupt; money is the root of all evil; the

bigger they are, the harder they fall—that particular constellation of moral clichés. But platitude or not, Cyrus's observation and the page that it informs ought not to be set aside as a simple (mechanical) gnome of closure. This is one of the greatest endings in ancient literature; it crystallizes all that precedes it in an astonishing way (the whole drama and dialectic of power in its complex movements in time and space gets caught up and knotted in these few simple words), and the voice of Cyrus has sounding beneath it the voice of Herodotus speaking to the Athenians who are the contemporaries of Sophocles, and beneath that voice resonates the voice of Dike speaking to everyone who has ever lived or will live.

What makes Cyrus's remark so shrewd, so irrefutable, is that it is very far from being a moral judgment. It is strictly practical and does nothing more than offer an opinion, which is based on a lifetime's rough and thorough experience, about what tends to result when certain choices are made. Cyrus doesn't say that it's pleasanter to rule than to be ruled, and he doesn't condemn the (understandable) desire to live comfortably. He merely points out that the habits that make people victors (a life in the saddle, a spare diet, little sleep, constant discipline) are essentially incompatible with ways of life whose patterns are pleasure, comfort, safety, repose, abundance. He doesn't suggest that the Persians would necessarily choose wrongly if they chose plentiful fresh fruits over less attractive army fare, but he knows what the Persians really value, and he senses that the temptations that victory brings with it may cause his countrymen to confuse what they value with what brings them unaccustomed, intense, and distracting delight. So he calls their attention to what is for them, in this time and this place, a (merely) obvious truth: they want power; that is, they want the freedom from the commands of others that power confers more than they want a steady, abundant supply of unnecessary pleasant extras, that is, the lesser fruits of victory. That is to say: if they settle into a pattern where enjoyment is more important to them than *askēsis,* than the physical and mental discipline that whets their hunger both for mere necessities and for victory, that enables them to seize victory when it comes their way, they will get out of shape, maybe permanently, and then, later, but maybe sooner, they may find themselves taking orders (once again). For them (in this situation), as for most humans (in various kinds of situations), then, now, anytime, the most obvious (sometimes bitter) truth is "No, you can't have it all, no, you can't have it both ways." These particular Persians, an audience that Cyrus knows well, agree with him that you can't have it all, can't have it both ways, and they desist (for the time) from entertaining notions of trading their small, rugged (and adequate) country for something larger, grander, gentler, kinder.

These Persians and their king show rare good sense in this passage, rare for them and rare for humankind. Indeed, the example is so exemplary that one is tempted to suppose that it is either a fiction that Herodotus has specially crafted for his closure or a fact that he has carefully burnished to a fictional brightness, again, for the purposes of closure. In either case, it is a closure that precisely "mirrors and echoes" his central scenes in the book, from Croesus to Xerxes, one that reminds the Athenians and us that though the myth of the unity of virtues invites us to forget it or otherwise to deny it, we all know, having been schooled by experience, that goods are almost always incompatible. The closure also suggests that, too often, unless grabbed by the scruff of the neck in time, we struggle to lose that truth, as if it were a tiresome caveat invented by the frail and fainthearted to ensure that the brave and the beautiful will not enjoy their birthright.

I recall this vivid Herodotean image of the dialectic of freedom, together with the sentimental response to it which tries to render it harmless by treating it as banal, because it offers us an approach to certain aspects of *Epistles 1* which also seem fated to be platitudinized.[1] *fuge magna,* "run from splendors," 10.32; *im-*

---

[1] What I'm calling the dialectic of freedom obviously hinges on the meanings the word had for Horace and his contemporaries. See Ste.-Croix's excellent discussion, 366–69, of recent trivializations of the word *libertas,* especially Syme's notorious neo-Hobbesian redefinitions, 368; see also

perat aut servit collecta pecunia cuique, "the cash he's hoarded either obeys him or enslave him," 10.47; *parvum parva decent,* "simple things suit simple people," 7.44; *nimirum hic ego sum—nam tuta et parvula laudo / cum res deficiunt,* that's me to a T—I praise what's safe and lowly when I'm short of cash, but when I strike it rich again, I go hog wild," 15.41–42; *qui metuens vivet, liber mihi non erit umquam,* "someone who lives in fear isn't free as far as I'm concerned," 16.66; *cena brevis iuvat et prope rivum somnus in herba,* "I like a light lunch and then a snooze in the grass on the riverbank," 14.35—such utterances seem to me to be too frequent in the *Satires* and in the *Odes* as well as in the *Epistles* to be the product of buzzwords of the *Zeitgeist* (largely inspired by Augustus's own ambiguous nostalgia) or to be mere literary conventions, strewn about his discourse as ornament and having no relation to the poet or his life or the world he lived in. The phrases, the sounds and images, that configure to create this Horatian version of the topos (the threat of abundance to freedom) seem rather to represent something crucial to Horace both as poet and as human being, something that in its frequency and its urgency in the poems seems almost an obsession with him throughout his career. Nor is this fixation on this topos naive or unexamined, whereas a not unsimilar fixation in Augustus and

---

Ste.-Croix's comments on Badian's contempt for the exploited and disenfranchised, 359, and on what "the rank-and-file" had in mind when they pondered the political, juridical, and economic connotations of the word, 334–37. Nicolet also offers illuminating discussions of what *libertas* meant to the individual in terms of how it bore on his legal and economic rights, 320–22; he provides a very useful treatment of the shift in emphasis of the word's center of gravity (from juridical to political), one in which the freedom to oppress others is of the essence for those with some degree of power, 322–24; and he gives an imaginative sketch of how the word is corrupted with the proliferation of bureaucracy and its own corruptions, 324–41—a subtler, in a sense more effective, form of repression than the political or judicial varieties, 326. For the centrality of freedom for the Cynics, see Kindstrand, 59–60; for Bion's notion of freedom, 62. Rudd, 66, 198–99 and 300 n. 52, writes well on varieties of freedom important to the Horatian varieties of it. For a discussion of the tensions between public and private freedom, see Lowe, 67–76.

some of his supporters *was* unexamined and, in the deepest sense of the word, sentimental, by which I mean characteristic of people who dislike or resent thinking about unpleasant truths so deeply that (systematically, as a cheerful style of perception) they try to view everything as through gauze (so the television commercial for car or cola or cat food) to make the consumption of reality easier, gilding whatever they encounter, as the occasion requires, with lyrical or nostalgic, patriotic or uplifting, tints.

Horace's version of pastoralism is, in Leo Marx's formulation, *complex,* not sentimental.[2] The ambivalence that structures one of his first full-scale explorations of the topos, *Epode* 2, remains with him all the way to C.4.15. Already in the early poem there is a raw yet effective irony where the usurer Alfius, as slippery a customer as any that Cato might have chosen to exemplify the profession, mawkishly intones the clichés of sentimental pastoralism and then, just when he is about to head off to his new farm (*iam iam futurus rusticus,* "Now, now that I'm about to become a genuine down-home kinda guy"), shows his true colors, gets cold feet and returns to Rome to pursue the career that nature intended him for. So, from the beginning, Horace was sensitive to the nature and the danger of a pastoralism that no irony had tempered, and in his wicked portrait of Alfius he gives a clear outline to his critical insight into the fears and unrealities and false hopes that even now nourish the enduring and archaic feelings whose whisper is "Yes, you can go home again (home to the farm, or if *you* weren't born there, then some anonymous ancestor or other was), and thereby you can escape paying the price for pursuing wealth and power, for evading 'the growing power and complexity of organized society' and thus give the lie to Freud and his grim cartoon of our urban discontents."

Yet if Alfius shows that this mood[3] is only, or is essentially, fantasy (as Juvenal's sad malcontent in his third satire will later show also), the Sabine farm and the freedom it represents remain

---

[2] Marx, 1964, 10–11, 69–72, 129–30.
[3] Marx, 1964, 226; Marx, 1988, 99–100.

equally and simultaneously a crucial part of Horace's imaginative world. The younger satirist may have exploded—or thought he did—the myth of a freedom won through flight from cosmopolitan anxieties, but, in his later transformation, the wry, aging *homme de lettres* finds that the idea of freedom cannot be laughed into oblivion. If we become dependent upon what maintains our leisure and well-being (which we can easily mistake for freedom), we may learn to adapt ourselves, almost without thinking about it, to a comfortable if very limited sort of freedom (or imitation of freedom) that is in fact as ambiguous and troubling as it is secure and prosperous. But when all is said and done, we can't live—so Horace says at the end of 1.16 to the king of Thebes—without hope that we may someday attain the (perhaps impossible) genuine freedom we all want (that is, need). What the force of Horace's complex dialectic of freedom shows is that we can't live honestly if, like Augustus and those whom he truly represents, we assume that a nation can become a world power (in this case, the known world's power) and not lose in the process of that transformation its claim to possess still intact an initial (if imaginary) integrity (here, the well-known rural simplicity); or, to put the matter a little less politically, Horace's dialectic of freedom shows that the individual cannot master or manipulate the complexity of cosmopolitan life *and* simultaneously live as if he were one of Cato's children, in the never-never land before the Second Punic War which Cato imagined so subtly and made the center of the Roman cultural code.

As a way of approaching their dialectic of freedom, let us look at the patterning of the poems in *Epistles 1*—or rather, let us look at the question of how the poems and their interdependent themes are configured in the volume they make up. Our ordinary habits of representing this sort of patterning are spatial or chronological or geometric, for mere instinct, perhaps sharpened by neoclassical conventions, prompts us to make diagrams or blueprints of what seems to be on the pages beneath our fingers and also in our brains as we read what the pages present us with. Thus Jean Préaux, whose readings of the poems have certainly influenced mine, sketches a neat "architecture" for the poems in which clusters of letters about *urbs* alternate with others about *rus* in elegant patterns (also involved in these alternations are *officium* and *otium* and an older generation of friends and a new generation of friends).[4] I'm convinced that this pattern is, almost, there in the poems and that it helps to explain much about what goes on in me when I'm reading the poems. But it also excludes much that I want to emphasize, and it tends to seem static, tends to freeze the tensions that rise up out of the poems' thematic discords and that produce reverberations that the closure of the book (to the extent that it can be said to have one) doesn't gather into stillness and unity.

How in fact do we read these poems? How can we go about describing the sort of structure-in-movement that they are possessed of? To get at the shape and meaning of our "modern" style of reading, let us imagine another, different kind of reading that contrasts with it. Think of some contemporary of the younger Pliny's, for instance. He calls to his *anagnostes* (the slave who reads aloud to his master, that living property, that walking compact-disc player, that breathing lexicon-encyclopedia, part classical actor, part consummate rhetorician-scholar), who "does" (performs) both Latin and Greek texts for him.[5] In a *Goldberg Variations* mood, unable to sleep, the master asks for Horace, *Epistles 1*. He specifies no particular poem, so the slave begins at the begin-

---

[4] Préaux, 3–8. Dilke, 1839–41, has some interesting suggestions about an extensive pattern of ring composition; Kilpatrick, xxiii, finds a complicated but plausible pattern of alternating young and old recipients. Kenney's remarks on "harmonious" structure are more compelling than his static scheme, 239.

[5] The significance, value, and functions of the *anagnostes* in Rome can be glimpsed between the lines (and without the lens of Macherey) in the fascinating letters from and to Cicero concerning his escaped information-storage-and-retrieval system, Dionysius, who may well have made it to freedom with the proceeds of his former master's library (*Fam.* 5.9–12, 13.77), and in the younger Pliny's not unpoignant and not unnaive letter about his Zosimus, which hints unawares at how much of Roman (and Greek) culture depended on "those" people.

ning and doesn't stop till he has read the last word of the twentieth poem, because his master, though he has found in the poems some ease from his distress, still cannot sleep, or because, though so diverted and relaxed that he could sleep, he fights sleep off to hear to the end the poems whose performance he has begun to enjoy so greatly. In less pressing circumstances, when the performances are to while away an hour or so or to entertain dinner guests and there is no time for the whole volume, specific poems will be requested. Sometimes the slave will not be summoned, perhaps, and the master and a friend (or he and a group of guests) will read to each other. Whatever the form of reading, with each new performance of the *Epistles,* whether the whole of it or parts of it, this reader-listener-performer, having heard (that is, ideally, listened to) the Horace volume performed both as a whole and in parts over a long period of time, having experienced its performance in the Latin it was written in (the language he was born into or acquired from native speakers), will find his ears remembering, almost before his brain does, a unity that his mind and feelings and imagination have cumulatively (palimpsestically) produced for it on all the occasions when he listened to its being performed from its text; this unity he carries about with him, waiting *in potentia,* an unfinished wholeness of this volume, something his memories, both intellectual and sensual, can reconstruct and further reorder both when he listens once again to the entire volume and (even) when, for some purpose, he unrolls the volume, hunts for a certain passage, finds it, and reads it, his lips barely moving, his voice barely audible, aloud to himself.

The reader I sketch here did not need to make diagrams of what the poem said (that is to say, abstract, spatial representations of the thoughts and feelings that his ears, nerves, and mind made of what he heard, the "meanings" he produced from what he listened to). True, if he was totally addicted to allegory, he might try to draw mental blueprints of the abstractions that his particular style of reading (instilled in him, probably, by his philosophical sect) empowered him to extract from the text and then plaster back on top of it. But for some and, given the aesthetic health of our classical pagan ancestors, perhaps even for many ancient readers, the allegorical chore was something one performed casually, by rote—because one had been trained to do it, because one could not break the habit of doing it—and then one got back as soon as possible to the pleasure of the sound of the performed text and its sensual (and intellectual) dynamics. The text, to these readers, meant many things, some of them relatively uniform throughout their listening experience, some of them changing drastically or very little; the text, their listened-to (not heard) text, though it remained, obviously, the same text in its physical state (unless miscopied or somehow tampered with), tended always, whether dramatically or imperceptibly, to change for them, *in* them, as their experience of reproducing it changed, whenever they listened to it being performed anew and heard the dynamics of its dialectical composition.

For us, who are usually silent readers (I know that some people hear abridgments of books—it is state-of-the-art pomo literacy—while they drive or jog or shop) and who have not much experience of the sort of intimacy with the poem that is got by being able to listen to it, for us, too, our poems exist *in potentia,* in the memory of the nerves as well as in the brain's memory, ready to be reconstructed when we reread them. For us, too, the poem exists both as a permanence (its physical text) and as something also changing with our new readings of it (our reproducing new meanings from the potentialities that await us both in the physical text and in our memories' versions the poem performed from that text). Yet when we want to try to talk not only about what the poem means but also about its ways of informing its thematic dialectics, we have recourse, almost inevitably, to diagrams of some sort which represent something static. We do this because we are (unconsciously) trying to make up for our inability to describe the feeling of producing meanings from the dynamics of a performed poem, because we are trying to recreate the *sense* of the poem we had in reading it by (and to) ourselves by trying to let ourselves see (fixed in space) a picture (one that is very inadequate and misleading) of what we hear and feel (in time) when we "perform" the poem in a silent and solitary performance. (I am assuming here, perhaps wrongly, that most of us on this continent in the late twentieth century seldom have the experience—poetry "readings" won't, usually, count here—of listening to someone read a sizable poem from its text to, or for, us. I suspect, moreover, that most of us do not even do very much in the way of reading aloud to ourselves.)

And even that abstract feel for the poem from the text, derived from a silent imitation of its performance, most of us can get only for poems written in our native language or in languages that we have learned to speak with some fluency. Most of us don't have it very readily with Latin or Greek (which is why we have such need of Stephen Daitz and Robert Sonkowsky, who are *not* trying to con us into thinking that they are reproducing those ancient sounds and who *are* trying to get us to use our vocal imaginations).[6] Our poetry in this century is a poetry of the printed page and of a reading that is silent; our ancient Greek and Latin poetry is a poetry of the printed page written in a dead language we have never heard and never will hear, and we first learn to read that poetry slowly, by decoding it with grammars, lexicons, textual apparatus, commentaries, books, and articles (and that primal experience, both for bad and good, stays stamped on the experience of the poems in question). I don't mean that we can never get to the point where we read this poetry and read it with genuine pleasure, for very obviously we do; I do mean that our understanding of our pleasure (something the critic should not be without) is doubly diminished in this regard, since we already tend to think about poetry as something

---

[6] One of the best contributions to the study of classics in the United States in the past few decades has been made by Stephen G. Daitz and Robert P. Sonkowsky with their series *The Living Voice of Greek and Latin* and in their workshops at the meetings of the American Philological Association in oral interpretation of ancient Greek and Latin literature. Their achievement was made possible by good technology in an age when much mediocre technology became really bad technology (there is, it can't be said too often, no neutral technology; if the elder Pliny knew that, why don't we?).

printed (not listened to) and, when we read Latin poetry, as something printed in a language that is available only in fragments and never heard (so, doubly silent). It is hard enough to imagine Pope or Wordsworth performed from their texts (recordings by famous actors are not always what the doctor ordered in these matters); even with Sonkowsky's help, wonderful as he is with ancient Latin poetry, to imagine the *Epistles* performed is difficult, because we have to imagine ourselves as fully competent to listen to (as against decode and then "read") them, because they are written in a dead foreign language that I, at least, will never know well enough, because, despite my interest in poems performed, my culture and my habits of reading and listening are not sufficient to the task. (I could say, to younger readers, that they might do well to watch/listen to MTV, where poetry that is not infrequently very good is sung—and in the case of African American raps [shades of Pindar!] sung and danced—and so get in the habit of experiencing good poetry performed from its texts and so perhaps bring that sensibility to the reading of ancient Greek and Latin poems. I could say that.)

How to treat of the structure of *Epistles 1* then? Ancient Latin is, let me imagine, in some sci-fi way, my native tongue, and I have absorbed the lesson of the rap lyricists and know how to describe (not recreate, that can't be done) my experience, my own reproduction of a poem when it is performed or when I read it and imagine it performed in an "ideal"(!) performance (that is, myself performing it my way with all the powers and gifts I lack in the ordinary and actual world). There is a circle, a revolving one . . . (Right back into the diagram, see? But this is a wobbly, decentered, unreliable circle; with this circle one tries to image dynamic motion, this one—enough excuses!) There is a revolving circle (it goes clockwise); it is made up of the poems addressed to Maecenas: 1, 7, 19 (here, almost, a sort of ring composition). Concentric inside it is another ring, revolving counterclockwise, this one composed of the poems to Lollius: 2 and 18. Between these two opposing rings, wavering, less stable far than they, are two further rings that are pulled, sometimes violently, now to the outer ring and now to the inner. They share some of their themes with each other as well as with the outer rings and so vibrate back and forth, through each other, from outer to inner, constantly unstable, constantly, in the tensions of the more stable rings and their countervailings, "looking for" a repose they cannot achieve.

One of these lesser rings, composed of letters 3, 6, 8, 9, 12, 13, and 16, has considerable thematic affinity with the Lollius ring. In these letters Horace discusses with his correspondents what interests *them* most: the design of the Roman hive, what makes its dreams tick (or buzz). It is in these letters that we find most of the volume's references to Augustus,[7] and these letters also allude to Agrippa and to Tiberius. Here, moreover, are to be found the most numerous and most dense configurations of images of prosperity and abundance. None of these letters, to my mind, shows much in the way of sparkle or verve—or of the affection that tends to mark the letters in its answering ring, which we will presently turn to. In fact, as a group, these are letters that Horace (or his fictive epistler) seems to have felt called upon to write, letters in answer to letters he wished he'd never received and would have preferred to have left unanswered, but couldn't or didn't. These are letters written by an ironically shallow social self to selves that are (essentially) purely public, purely social.

Letters 4, 5, 10, 11, 14, 15, and 17 make up the second lesser ring, whose essential kinship is with the Maecenas ring. These poems are written to friends. In them a private self shows varying degrees of affection to his correspondents and offers them some degree of warmth and intimacy. Moreover, in addition to a tendency to echo and reinforce the thematics of the Maecenas letters, this group also, on balance, counters the thematics of the

---

[7] The big exception to this is letter 5, to Torquatus, where Augustus's birthday celebration without his presence offers an occasion for some heavy boozing and good drunken chatter (9–11, 19–20; the context of inebriated public/private discourse recalls also, for example, the closure of the fourth book of the lyrics). See also Allen et al., 1970, 255; Préaux, 16; Kilpatrick, xxiii; Mayer, 1985, 44.

other lesser ring and of the Lollius ring. It is in these letters that the imagery of farm and country tends to cluster most densely and to challenge the imagery of the imperial cosmopolis and the often lethal prosperity that characterizes both the ring of public selves and the Lollius ring.[8]

The Maecenas ring is composed of letters to his friend and "patron" which concern themselves with the ambiguities of patronage, with what it means to be a poet, and with the indeterminacies of the links between the poet's autonomy and his art; but, despite the confused anger these poems don't quite suppress, these are poems to a friend, to the human being who means more to the poet than anyone else, to the person by whose side he sees to it that he will be buried. The Lollius ring, on the other hand, consists of poems addressed to a young man who, son (or nephew) of a very recent consul though he is, needs help in establishing himself in certain influential circles, needs help in learning to become a successful protégé. The tone of these letters seems to me mixed at best. I detect a certain amount of sympathy (perhaps) in 2 (affection it is not), but the moods and gestures of 18 are, on balance, rather cooler, a little more impatient, show a bit more in the way of studied avuncularity. One is tempted to think that Lollius represented for Horace, at least in part, an aspect of himself, an *istantanea* of himself taken when he was this young man's age and one he'd like to forget—a faded portrait of the young artist on the make. For Horace, Lollius represented a "negative identity fragment" seen in the rearview mirror. If there is a very slight, real story behind these two letters, it might have to do with an older, successful poet who took time out to assist a younger, struggling writer, gave him some good advice, wrote a

---

[8] Letter 16 to Quinctius might seem an exception here, but though it begins with the fullest description of the farm we have, it quickly shifts to the bondage that prosperity brings with it, and it ends with a somber recreation of the *Bacchae* and with defiance of what seeks to destroy freedom. Quinctius is, moreover, also the recipient of *C*.2.11, a tough and ironic attack on those who waste their time chasing after "security" by chasing after abundance.

few letters in his behalf, and then found the young man back on his doorstep again, pretending to ask for more advice, though what he in fact wanted, as was now painfully clear, were better introductions and bigger secrets about how to make it big.

What is substance in the Maecenas poems is shadow in the Lollius poems. The young man looks at Horace's life and art and sees glitter and triumph. Horace looks at his own life and art (at this moment or this fictive moment of his life and career, as you choose, but maybe best choose a mix of the two) and what he sees there are his failed freedom as an artist and as a human being and the barely visible, tangled forces (inside the poet and outside him) that work together to spoil art and corrupt its truth; what he thinks he sees (in the poems at least) is a damaged, partial, wasted life. These are the antinomies (what Lollius sees as against what Horace sees) between which the thematics in the other poems reverberate; it is out of this complex, irresoluble dialectic that the dynamics of the volume is engendered.

And what's at the center of the circle? Maybe the volume's closure (closures) that fails (fail) to close it. Suppose that circle becomes (at times) a cone gyring from its base (up and down, shades of Willie!) through its vertex when poem 20 fuses with poem 10 (the volume's other center, in which its collisions *are,* briefly, resolved—before they begin again) to reform and to refigure itself and its "stillness-in-tumult" below and above, on the other side. Poem 20, "addressed" by the poet to the volume itself, mimes, in its freedom from most of the volume's thematic patternings (and obsessions), which it is literally on the verge of being beyond, its own variation on the book's central theme, namely, freedom, even as it counterpoints the cry for freedom in the first poem, in exact symmetry. In 1, Horace asks Maecenas for his freedom, for release from service (he is, of course, free, but he is not free from fears about unfreedom, and he is not free from doubts about what to do with his life, about how to escape from, to be free from, those fears: his request is, as he indicates at the close of the poem, neurotic, irrational—but it is not unreal or unreasonable). In 20, the tables are turned. Here as in S.2.7, he is

[69]

faced with a request for freedom from *his* slave, this young (new) poetry book, which he irritably and grudgingly yields to: "OK, you silly little faggot. Go off and peddle your ass in the streets of Rome and see how much you like that. You'll be sorry—and soon, too—when you find yourself missing your kindly protector, who really loves you, when you realize how very good to you he really was." What the boybook is actually thinking about, perhaps, is all the pleasure it will give and all the admiration it will find itself deliciously drowning in. It doesn't yet understand how often it will be abused (and misprized), how persistently it will háve to scatter its anxiety-making influences over the long centuries, not to mention how it will have to schlepp its way through monkish libraries and used and sometimes even new bookstores. What it intuits, maybe, is that it will contrive to retain its youth when most much younger books have lost all theirs, and, despite its author's fears for it, it guesses that it will know how to take care of itself. The hustler boybook, abandoning his love-master/slave, zooms off into its own comic utopia (a truly funny noplace) away from the dreary world where patrons and protégés, urbanists and ruralists, technocrats and idlers, all enact their silly word games of artistic freedom and social constraint, of the claims of genius and the facts of rampant law and order.

This final affirmation of freedom, not for the poet, of course, who can never really be free, but for his poems, which must be free, reprises the initial, desperate demand for emancipation which Horace made to Maecenas in 1, and transforms it (so, another ring composition). The poems between 1 and 20 will examine various aspects of the dialectic of freedom/unfreedom and will tend to suggest, in their accumulated moods and fancies, in their total, rather (deliberately) messy ensemble effects, that pure freedom is an illusion, that immaculate freedom is not really possible *ici bas* (though one doubts that Horace would let this be taken as a warrant for various kinds of disenfranchisement and oppression). But in 20, suddenly freedom is possible—for the young hustler in his escape to the great world (*he,* as opposed to his maker, is filled with fresh illusions and fresh energies, is, in a way, not unlike the hilarious, escaping bird bard, the goofy Pindaric swan, of C.2.20).[9] This is a violent, comic denouement (a sort of Priapus *ex machina,* the love-slave set free) to a set of dialectical tensions that will allow of no real or serious resolutions (because there is no "solution" to the problem of incompatible goods; there are only particular choices that create new contexts for new problems; that is to say, there is only "living"). In *E.2.2,* from another book with another set of moods and fancies, another slightly more serious version of something like freedom and the (temporary yet genuine) serenity it can bestow will be offered (see above, pp. 1–3). But here the poet in whom the satirist is seldom far from the surface and never absent from the core decides that his collection can and indeed must explode into delicious laughter.

Iccius, the recipient of 12, Horace's readers have encountered before, in C.1.29, *Icci, beatis nunc Arabum invides / gazis.* In that brief lyric, as in this brief letter, Iccius is (he claims) deeply engrossed in his philosophical studies, though he has (in the lyric), to what Horace claims is his surprise, temporarily packed away all his Stoic and Platonic texts to go off to the East and make some money by pacifying the savages and bringing them (in obedience to Mommsen's law) the very mixed blessings of Roman civilization. In the *Epistles,* now in charge of Agrippa's Sicilian estates, Iccius apparently manages (unlike Democritus, who couldn't do two things at once, 12–13) to perform his official duties without giving up his philosophical endeavors. For all that, busy though he is at his job *and* at his avocation (or hobby, perhaps), Iccius is no happier now with his financial situation than he was when the ode was written to him (at him). Horace therefore takes up his pen once again to offer consolation for this new disappointment and to offer the amateur philoso-

---

[9] See Hirt, 36–37, and Anthony, 115, for the epistle; for C.2.20, see Johnson, 1966.

pher a little more dry advice. The tone of the letter is one of friendly banter. Iccius and Horace had become acquainted with each other, and the young man wanted Horace's friendship, and Horace found something attractive in Iccius (if only the droll, rather touching, not really silly discrepancy between his eagerness to strike it very rich and his less vigorous though doubtless genuine need to make some sense of life with the help of philosophical aids). What the lyric offers is a kind of Cubist portrait of Iccius as sundered personality, and he is not, in this regard, as other odes show, an isolated phenomenon in early Augustan Rome as far as the poet is concerned. Recall the outrageous (yet decorously commonplace) hyperbole at 10–12: *quis neget arduis / pronos relabi posse rivos / montibus et Tiberim reverti.* "If you give up your expensive editions of Panaetius and various post-Socratic pundits," the poet writes, "in order to put on military regalia and go off to fight in rich Arabia, who would be willing to admit that rivers couldn't flow backwards up steep mountains and the Tiber itself turn itself around?—so committed did you seem to the pursuit of wisdom!" To see him speed off to where the cash was said to be clinking was not, the banal hyperbole tells us, very much like watching a leopard change its spots; the change of heart was predictable and probably predicted. The poet had guessed that the amiable young man had not much drive to master the syllogism and the excluded middle. The ode tells us that its poet was charmed and amused by the naiveté and the misguided zest—and by the untapped, enviable energies.

But the verse letter to the same young man is another matter. What delighted a few years back is not so delightful anymore. Horace has changed, Iccius has not—or has, perhaps, but only for the worse. So, though the letter is civil, it is implacable: *tolle querellas,* "Quit the whining!" 3. *pauper enim non est, cui rerum suppetit usus,* "He isn't badly off who has enough to get along; he has enough who has—enough." Then some avuncular home truths, not much softened for their recipient by the gleam of their wit. One aspect of that wit is the emphasis on what seems to be, by his own report, fascinating Iccius at the moment: in the ode he had seemed, *socratice,* concerned with ethics, but now he's got into the heavy stuff: science, physics, cosmology, you know— *concordia discors,* that ontologically significant, cosmically discordant symphony (*Ars poetica* 374). The Cynic in Horace—he is as available to him as the Epicurean self, defusing dogma with doubt, reinforcing the huge distrust of power and power's jungle of codes—is amused by a man who, failing to understand what the simplest fisherman could tell him something about—how to live simply and honesty—wants to know (in his spare time, when he's not busy with his abacus) the really big picture and what's really behind it all: the face behind "the masks of the cosmos."[10] OK, pal. Go learn the secrets of the universe (since, apparently, you're not bright enough to learn what those who are too poor to learn to read struggle to learn because they must— how to try to live). And while you're at it, be nice to my good chum, your neighbor down there in Sicily, Grosphus, whenever he pops in for a visit. You two should get along swell together.

Grosphus is the recipient of the splendid ode 2.16, one of the crucial poems in the first lyric collection, where *vivitur parvo bene,* "life is well lived when frugally lived" (13) shines forever radiant, foiled as it is by the ferocious cartoons of greed, fear, and self-loathing that surround it, reprised as it is in the inimitable closure: *mihi parva rura et / spiritum Graiae tenuem Camenae / Parca non mendax dedit,* "Fate that does not lie gave me a few acres and the delicate breath of the Latin Muse," 37–39, *et malignum / spernere vulgus,* "and gave me a further gift, to scorn the mean-spirited (and materialistic) majority," 39–40. Here we have another possible motto for the *Epistles,* one that contains within it

[10] For the tone of the letter, see Kilpatrick, 84; he finds it the "most complex" of the letters, "a mixture of irony, friendly humor and gentle earnestness." For the influence of the Cynics on the poems, see Moles, 34 (*E.*1.2); Malherbe, 1977, 6, 7, 144, who thinks that "The Letters of Diogenes" seem to have been written in the late first century B.C. (letter 19, with its nose-thumbing *pros ton "autos epha" legonta* is characteristic); they show considerable interest in freedom/slavery topoi, 94, 98, 102, 104, 106, 112.

the seeds of discontent, the dialectical pressures, that will blossom into the *Epistles*. The mention of Grosphus (and his pairing with Iccius) triggers emotions that the controlled irony earlier in the letter had brushed aside (emotions centered on the dangers of a little too much prosperity, about the fragility of a freedom whose foundations we have ceased to reexamine, to keep in good repair). With *verum seu piscis seu porrum et caepe trucidas,* "whether you butcher a fish or only leeks and onions," 21, in preparation for giving Grosphus a dinner, the control wobbles. *trucidas* is a sort of hidden zeugma that joins not only the rich fish with the poor vegetables but also the pretensions and hypocrisy of Iccius (a yearning for the elemental truths and the simple life) with the insatiable greed (which is maybe greater than Iccius's) of Grosphus. Here is your true teacher, Grosphus, who cannot comprehend being satisfied with what he has. He will seek out only what is *verum et aequum,* 23 (*aequum,* that sacred word for Horace, as in *aequus animus*), but only in the financial sense, not in the philosophical one (for that you can always go to Stertinius, 20, and his rigorous, rationalizing, comforting banalities; you probably prefer him to Empedocles and his dialectical, messy, disturbing truths: *concordia discors*). Grosphus is an honest businessman, he'll give you good deals, you won't regret getting to know him and doing business with him—*und so weiter*. Not what Horace is looking for, not what he's interested in.

Then comes a staggering yet utterly decorous *Stimmungsbruch*. Iccius is way off in Sicily; maybe he doesn't get the fresh news freshly (a little parody here perhaps of Ciceronian epistolary convention?).[11] Horace gives Iccius a précis of everything big that's happened recently in the cosmic empire. Agrippa has smashed Cantabria, and Armenia has capitulated to Tiberius. Phraates, on his knees in humility and humiliation, now recognizes Augustus as his master (*ius imperiumque Phraates / Caesaris acceptis genibus*

---

[11] For useful remarks on Horace's spare use of epistolary conventions, see Dilke, 1837–38; for useful observations on some of the conventions themselves, see Gamberini, 337–57. See also Frischer, 92–95.

minor, 27–28) and is shorter than Augustus, because he's down on his knees—is that the most graceful way to say it? Then a ravishing epic sentiment, written in sublime *Schlagsahne: aurea fruges / Italiae pleno defundit Copia cornu,* "The Golden Abundance of Italy from her overflowing Horn spills forth her Fruits." (So, a few years later in the *Carmen saeculare, apparetque beata pleno / copia cornu,* 59–60, making what seems a slightly less glamorous appearance, she is forced to share the spotlight with Faith and Peace and Honor and *priscus* Shame and *neglecta* Virtue, who is here making her comeback.) The parade float is just as Augustus wants it. But not the way Horace wants it. How he wants it is sketched in *E.*10.

Aristius Fuscus is already well known to us both from *S.*1.9, where he made the famous refusal to save Horace from the infamous bore, and from *C.*1.22, where he, *urbanissimus,* is comically regaled with the glories of country living (rural wolves love poets, or at least they are sufficiently afraid of their sacred powers to flee them rather than attack them) in what I take to be an affectionately ironic invitation to spend some time in the country—which Fuscus, as Horace knows very well, happens to loathe. Taken together, these poems adumbrate the funny yet serious conflict between these close friends which this verse letter dramatizes.

One of the disadvantages of being a famous person in the crowded metropolis Horace catches in amber in *S.*1.9, his encounter with the bore. Though he is adequately gregarious (but not much with strangers or near strangers, and perhaps if he doesn't call you friend, you might as well be a stranger to him), Horace likes to stroll about the city by himself (see above, p. 23). He doesn't like being recognized; he doesn't like being ambushed by fans or self-seekers masquerading as fans. One gathers that for Fuscus, who is probably not so well known as Horace and is therefore less vulnerable to groupies both sincere and insincere, even this flaw in metropolitan living seems to have a certain charm—it may represent for him some of the hectic yet exhilarating give-and-take that comes with urban living. Horace is citified, certainly, and, as we saw hints of in *Epode 2,* his pastoralism is destined to remain, for all its changes, ironic and complex; yet he seems to have grown more partial to the country in proportion as he has grown hypersensitive—or just sensitive—to the disadvantages of Augustan Rome (*beatae / fumum et opes strepitumque Romae,* C.3.29.11–12, which represents both physical discomfort and a kindred spiritual pollution). In C.1.22 the hyperbole of the return to paradise is laid on with a trowel just to give Fuscus a little fun. For his friend's delight he parodies pastoralism (and the poetic shamanism its sentimental versions tend to favor) by setting himself smack in the middle of the antique, artificial Eden—holy poet, holy lover, man of perfected virtue, living the old-time, pristine, unspoiled life, there in his willow cabin where he and his Lalage gaze up from each other—into the ornate mirrors on the bedroom ceiling. Fuscus was doubtless quite pleased with this send-up of cloying Arcady: the temporarily demented supersophisticate impersonating the noble savage, terrifying fatal beasts, playing hovel with his sweetie, and warbling his woodnotes wild.

I expect that Fuscus was no less pleased with *E.*10, one of the most accessible of the letters, both for its condensed vigor and for its delicacy of feeling. This is a poetic memorial to what may well have been a real debate between two friends who saw eye to eye on most matters, but not on this one; like twins with truly fraternal hearts, when one says no, so does the other (*hac in re scilicet una / multum dissimiles, at cetera paene gemelli / fraternis animis—quidquid negat alter et alter,* 2–4). Then the brilliant, the unforgettable, touch: *adnuimus pariter vetuli notique columbi,* "We nod in agreement like two old, familiar doves." The debate between them is not rendered fully and fairly, since we have only Horace's side of it, but the jist of Fuscus's argument can perhaps be reconstructed from Horace's strategies in countering it. I offer a sample of what that argument might be: "Why do you keep disappearing off to that ramshackle dump with no running water and yucky food and crummy wine and no one to talk to? I know—you want peace and quiet. You can have peace and quiet when you go out the door feet first under Libitina's protection.

And you can have peace and quiet right here in Rome if you want to. You could live in a quieter part of town; you could live anywhere you want to, any way you want to. It's a bummer having you always cutting out to the country. Screw the country—your place is here. And who will you try your poems out on, stuck way out there in the boonies? Read 'em to the trees like Vergil's dumb shepherds maybe? Maybe recite them to your wolf chums? Why not get your act together and settle down easy, right here, in the best damn city west of Alexandria? What's bugging you anyhow?"

What's bugging Horace, he reveals when he provides the moral to the fable of the horse who helps humans get rid of its own enemy, the stag, only to find itself enslaved by its new "ally": *sic qui pauperiem veritus potiore metallis / libertate caret, dominum vehet improbus atque / serviet aeternum, quia parvo nesciet uti*, "thus because he was afraid of being poor, a man ends up bereft of his freedom, which is worth more than money, and this sick, crazy bastard will end up lugging a master around on his back as long as he lives because he didn't know how to make the best of modest circumstances," 39–41. If a person's situation doesn't suit him (*cui non convenit sua res*), it's the way it often is with shoes (*ut calceus olim*)—if they're too big for him, they trip him up; if they're too small, they pinch him (*si pede maior erit, subvertet, si minor, uret*). *res* here means money, but it also means his place in the world, and how he feels in his skin. There's something in Horace, in his temperament, in how he's made, that Fuscus happens not to be afflicted with.

"I really begin to live, I feel like a king, the moment I've left behind me (*vivo et regno simul ista reliqui*, 8) what you praise to the skies (*quae vos ad caelum effertis*, 9), and, like a runaway slave (*utque sacerdotis fugitivus*, 10), I despise the sacred cakes (*liba recuso*): what I need right now is good plain bread (*pane egeo iam*, 11)."[12] Horace is insisting here that life and complete autonomy

---

[12] For *convenit* (in the preceding paragraph), see Cic. *Off.* 1.110; *tamen nos studia nostra nostrae naturae regula metiamur; neque enim attinet naturae repugnare nec quicquam sequi, quod assequi non queas;* 112: *atque haec differentia naturarum*

are synonymous. *regno—rex erit qui recte faciet.* From Fuscus's point of view, that need to control everything is doubtless, to put it kindly, nutty; to put it less kindly, it is a sick, neurotic need, grounded in a fear that finds expression in obsessive efforts to self-dramatize alienation and fantasize into reality what in Fuscus's eyes is an illusory, impossible independence, one that can be achieved only by running away (*fugitivus*) from civilization and its discontents. (*fugitivus,* here at the center of the collection, is an echo of the gladitorial image of the first poem and of its *latet abditus agro,* and it looks forward to the boybook escapee of the final poem.) Instead of cakes and ale, a plain loaf. From Fuscus's point of view, perhaps, that is melodramatic, hysterical, hyperbolical, insincere: I need to eat bread, not cake. Why not, he might ask, eat both? you can afford to, you have the choice. Melodramatic it may seem, but insincere it is not.

To say that Fuscus seems to have been able to make accommodation with the moral dangers of the city is in no way to discredit his choice or to denigrate him. The city's moral dangers (put in another way, its unpleasant features) are in his mind (and very possibly in fact) compensated for by its diversity, its capacity for circumventing expectation, its superb excesses. This willingness to balance defects with virtues of defects derives not as much from rational effort as it does from temperamental predisposition (as Horace himself confesses with his image of shoes that fit and don't fit), and this awareness of varieties of temperament is of the essence for Horace's poetry. Fuscus's instinct for tolerance, moreover, for accepting, even delighting in, what is other, what is contrary to his values and preferences, and his ability to adapt himself to happenstance (the bore, for instance) and master it (in life, not only in art) are qualities that Horace wants to import into himself (from Fuscus). Or rather, it is at least a mask (of the Yeatsian, not the Poundian, kind) that he

---

tantam habet vim; 113: *id enim maxime quemque decet, quod est cuiusque maxime suum;* for *regno,* 70; *his idem propositum fuit quod regibus . . . cuius proprium est, sic vivere ut velis.*

wants for his poetry, and one that in the closure of *E.2.2* (and maybe in life, but that is not within our competence and none of our business) he achieves.

Such acceptance of things as they are, such cheerfulness in the face of uncertainty, are in fact qualities that many of us would give to our personal composites of Horace—because he persuades us that this attitude is a useful one, one that is adequate to our needs, one that, irrespective of what meanings it might have in a system of pure ethics, he himself lives by. But in the *Epistles,* such an attitude, though it has made dim appearance as something admirable in the lyrics, is here something one strives after, perhaps as long as one lives, without ever quite attaining it. It is not something that Horace can lay claim to (perfectionist that he is, mercurial as he is, irritable as he is). But Fuscus, who loves the city and its perils and surprises, does possess this attitude, and here the foil figure, the opposite that attracts and challenges and thus defines one's identity, here Fuscus becomes a model, for Horace wants to be a little more like Fuscus than he is. In the context of the *Epistles,* however, he can't yet be more like Fuscus. Here, between the fake Eden and the hazards of the city, here is no real choice. But he chooses, or claims to choose, the country, with its mild climate and its distance from the smoke and the lucre of Rome and all the corruption and servitude that go with them. The man who is afraid of being poor has given up all his freedom for a security that seemed equivalent to or inclusive of "enough" freedom. It is riches (not *pauperies,* which is "very modest means," not "poverty") and what they bring with them that are to be feared, for anyone who fears *not being rich* or *being rich no more* has in fact lost his freedom, because he doesn't understand what it is he needs, doesn't understand that he can free himself *from* fear if he works hard to see reality, things as they are, and in doing this enters into the process of becoming free *for* joy in his life and in the mysteries and beauties of the inscrutable universe (*rerum concordia discors*) of which he happens, for a time and for the eternal present, to be part.

Fuge magna! The horse that wanted mere safety (that is, that

wanted the stag not able to compete with it for food) and therefore enlisted human help against its obvious rival ended by en-
slaving itself by destroying its enemy. Better to have endured the
original, unequal rivalry with the stag or to have moved off to
another grazing place than to have fallen victim to the illusion
that one can secure one's comforts (or happiness) without paying
some price for that security. *imperat aut servit collecta pecunia
cuique, / tortum digna sequi potius quam ducere funem,* "The money
we have amassed is for each of us a tyrant or a servant, but money
ought to follow the rope that secures the neck, not drag the hand
that holds the rope," 47–48. Is money, then, neutral, as weapons
throughout history or our current technologies are said to be?
Perhaps; but as Lucretius's sketch of the progress of "technique"
suggests, the tendency seems to be toward unintended consequences and incompatible goods. The image of the twisted rope
recalls the puppet on the string of *S*.2.7 as well as the enduring
fetters of the greedy horse. Money, here as elsewhere, is a real
threat to freedom, but it is also symbolic of a wider realm of
abundance and security, of an unreal serenity that seduces us into
lazy habits of needless comfort and makes us reluctant or even
unwilling to return to face difficulties and toil should the need
arise. Flabby and slothful, we trade small freedom after small
freedom, one after the other, to maintain the fiction of freedom
from want. It is only when our liberty is in ruins and our dependency has become too clear to permit of further disguise of it,
further euphemisms for it, that, like the horse, we see what it is
that rides us. Horace feels, acutely, the discrepancy between
what he has and what he is, between what he thinks he needs and
what he needs to become. Fuscus has learned, apparently, to fit
himself to things as they are (see *E*.1.19). This means, of course,
at this moment in Horace's crisis, problems for their friendship.
But the measure of the strength of that friendship and their
regard for; each other are those abrupt, enchanting two verses
that close the letter to Fuscus: *haec tibi dictabam, post fanum putre
Vacunae, / excepto quod non simul esses, cetera laetus,* "I'm dictating
this letter behind Vacuna's crumbling shrine, perfectly happy,

except for the fact that you're not here with me." He may feel happy at this moment (as he imagines himself at this moment) because of the peace and seclusion of the place, but maybe that awareness of this instant of happiness stems from his having been talking—long-distance—with one of the dearest of his few close friends.[13]

In contrast to all that Fuscus, the city lover, values, his own version of the *locus amoenus,* the charming, the real good place, may well take on special grace and meaning right now as he defends himself to Fuscus. But the book of poems of which this letter is the center hardly shows a uniform radiance or calm. What he rejects here (the city and what it symbolizes) is never very far from his mind in the poems that compose this book. His conflict with Fuscus, which is also, in a different and much more powerful manifestation, a conflict inside himself, is not something that he can argue away, can argue himself out of, or argue out of himself. His identity, particularly in this poem and in the book that is centered on it, is shaped by both the necessity and the impossibility of freedom (as well as by the necessity for—and maybe the impossibility of—the interdependence and fusion of the contrary virtues that city and country represent).

So, he is not lying to Fuscus when he says *cetera laetus,* nor is he exactly trying to delude himself, trying to prove his case to Fuscus and to himself with a rabbit pulled from a hat: See, I'm truly happy here, away from Rome. He believes he's happy, at this moment, and at this moment it is true—in writing the letter, in rearranging the antinomies by a friendly debate with an absent Fuscus, he has persuaded himself that he should, could, must be, is happy. But as we see elsewhere throughout the letters, and particularly in the next one, 11, and then again in 15, which just precedes the complex trio 16, 17, 18, where the dialectic of freedom gathers furious momentum, this kind of moment, the clarity of happiness (the instant of equilibrium), is rarer far than he wants it to be, than he expected it to be when he first tried to

---

[13] For Vacuna, see Macleod, 1979, 27.

make (began to dream of making) his retirement in the country permanent. Such moments don't last long, and they can't quite escape (in his own understanding of them) the charge of being both transitory and illusory until the conflicts between freedom and abundance (= dependency), between vitality (city) and serenity (country), between freedoms that are inner and freedoms that are outer, can be resolved. And in this book, this collection of letters written from inside these conflicts, the conflicts are never resolved, at least not before our very eyes (mimetically, narratologically). But, as I suggest in the following chapter, it is possible for the conflicts to be refigured, or ways to refigure them can be discovered and then gestured toward, in times and places *later,* outside the poems, outside poetry.

Still, if there is no resolution in the book as a whole or in 1.10, between the friends there is reconciliation. *excepto quod non simul esses,* "except that you're not here with me." "Having a wonderful time, wish you were here" can seldom have found an incarnation more precise in its tact and delicacy. Laconic tenderness lifts the poem to a rare moment (rare in these poems) of lyric revelation, and the image of Vacuna, which foreshadows the gaudy goddess two poems ahead, Golden Cornucopia (patroness of shopping malls), strewing on the imperial self her ill-gotten harvest with mindless benevolence, gathers the poem into its complex balance. Vacuna (maybe a Sabine goddess of victory, but in Horace's time a goddess of holiday, of vacation—*vacuus,* free, *otium,* caprice) belongs to another order of living than that over which Copia holds sway. Simplicity, sufficiency, time to reflect: an older order of things, another realm of being, where leisure had meaning because work was (as Cato had insisted, almost Hesiodically) the root of goodness, of justice, of truth, that is, of what had real meaning. But her shrine, of course, is in ruins. This is a lovely (almost Romantic) place. Green nature, almost nature as praised by Pliny the Elder, shines around him in the sunlight that reveals how proud man's endeavors to oppress and transform her to his own image—Triumph and Progress— have failed: *naturam expelles furca, tamen usque recurret, / et mala perrumpet firtum fastidia victrix*, 24–25 (a nice reprise to his jab at Fuscus about his citified, rather sentimental, and very extravagant taste in exterior decoration, 22–23). A quiet, beautiful spot, well suited to contemplation (and even dictation), but, alas, not quite real, not in terms of the larger world that Horace has fled from. Vacuna is in ruins: Horace's tough pastoralism will not permit him to say *cetera laetus* without adding this touch of countertruth. Yet crumbling though her shrine is, this goddess of Victory in ruins, this goddess of caprice, is peculiarly Horatian, and she points him toward the great prayer of *E.*1.18, which, as we're about to see, marks his awareness of what his (and our) integrations might consist of.

[4]

DECORUMS

If ten pounds are too much for a particular person to eat and
two too little, it does not follow that the trainer will offer six
pounds; for this is also too much for the person who takes it, or
too little—too little for Milo, too much for the beginner in
athletic exercises. . . . Thus a master of any art avoids excess
or defect but seeks the intermediate and chooses this—the
intermediate not in the object but relatively to us.

So much, then, is plain, that the intermediate state is in all
things to be praised, but that we must incline sometimes to the
excess, sometimes to the deficiency: for so we shall most easily
hit the mean and what is right.
                              —Aristotle, *Nicomachean Ethics* 2.6 and 9

Just ten lines into *E*.1, having asked Maecenas for his freedom
(the question, the demand, is at once rhetorical, ironical, hypothetical, and even, in a way, maybe genuine), Horace goes on to
tell him what he will be using this newfound freedom for:

quid verum atque decens, curo et rogo et omnis in hoc sum,
condo et compono quae mox depromere possim.
ac ne forte roges quo me duce, quo lare tuter,
nullius addictio iurare in verba magistri,
quo me cumque rapit tempestas, deferor hospes.

11–15

I'm concerned about, I ask everyone about [rather like Socrates, please note], in short, I've given myself wholly up to—surprise!—what's true and what's proper. I'm laying in everything I manage to lay my hands on that I think I can maybe make use of at some later date [the image here is from the wine cellar, as befits a not very orthodox Epicurean]. And just so you won't have to ask me whom I'm studying ethics with, in what school I've enrolled, the answer is, I haven't signed up with anybody, I owe allegiance to no master. When I travel philosophically, buffeted about as I am by my inner hurricanes, my motto is "Any port in a storm."

That doesn't sound very much like heroic spiritual journeying, but there is worse to come: *nunc agilis fio et mersor civilibus undis,* "Now I become public-spirited and plunge into (and am drowned by) the rough waters of civic duty"—*virtutis verae custos rigidusque satelles,*"I, the protector, the fanatic bodyguard of True Virtue," 16–17 (perhaps he has in mind here the misreadings of the Roman odes, based on the equation Flaccus = Cato the Elder, which were apparently already getting ready to creep into the schoolroom and its commentaries). A little out of character, perhaps, this claim to be a pillar of society from the carnal, manic-depressive ironist? But what's really outrageous is the bland admission, the casual confession: *nunc in Aristippi furtim praecepta relabor, / et mihi res, non me rebus subiungere conor,* "Now suddenly I have a relapse and find myself listening, in clandestine fashion, to the precepts of Aristippus [*praecepta* is precisely and ironically *not* the mot juste for the genial avuncularities of Aristippus], and I try to bend the world to me and my ways [Horace might have liked the word "life-style" to have some fun with] instead of trying to fit myself to nature and to reality."

The bipolarity here, implacable Stoic versus effete Cyrenaic, is probably meant to be symbolic of the entire philosophical spectrum. But since the Stoics are invoked throughout the letters (never without a shade of irony somewhere about) as exemplars of virtue and moral manhood, and, as we'll presently see, Aristippus makes a final, unexpected, and very favorable appearance in the book (*E.*17), at a dramatic and crucial moment, the opposition, beyond its formal and symbolic economy, perhaps defines a conflict, a problem, that Horace took personally—that is to say, the opposition represents, at the opening of the book, one of the book's major themes. *agilis fio, rigidus, verae virtutis custos?* Even if *agilis fio* means something like "I sometimes write what appears to the unwary reader to be patriotic verses," these uncharacteristic pompities—the lyric honeybee or *papillon de Parnasse* has become a soldier for Virtue?—strain one's suspension of disbelief to the snapping point. But the affirmation of occasional, furtive dalliances with Aristippus suits admirably with very much of what goes on in the *Satires* and in the first lyric collection. Whatever he is or isn't, Horace is certainly a faithful, practicing hedonist. His testament to Aristippus rings true, whereas his confession of the Porch doesn't.

But what this passage is essentially concerned with is Horace's autonomy. His claim to autonomy (I'm my own man) is ironically (but not insincerely and not quite untruly) phrased as if his inability to stick to one school were the result of his radical instability of character. But, as we gather elsewhere, mostly from *E.*18, he is incapable of staying in one school and of becoming and remaining an adherent of any orthodoxy, because no closed system has all that he needs, that is, no system is true in each of its links or contains all truth *for him*. (This view doesn't make of Horace a relativist or even one of those limp eclectics that haunt the neocon's nightmares; it makes of him a healthy—not morbid—skeptic whose skepticism cuts both ways almost always; that is to say, it makes of him a pluralist.) It is not only because the human mind and its languages are not big enough to contain the realities around them (much less the realities beyond them) but also because human beings differ so markedly from one another (even as they are so very similar to one another) that no master or group can embrace truth that will be sufficient or suitable for everyone.[1] Moreover, human beings are themselves,

---

[1] Armstrong, 117–19, has interesting thoughts on this temperamental aspect of "philosophy," but if he is correct in seeing that Horace was joking when he said he had begun to study philosophy in his "old age," he seems on thinner ice when he assumes that Horace "relies on" or "turns the study of"

each of them, so radically variable that what suits the individual in one circumstance may not suit her in another, what is beneficial in one configuration of contingencies and volitions may turn out to be less than useless in another.

Verum et decens, the true and the adequate, is not something that you go and get from teachers or books or both. It is more nearly like something that you piece together for yourself from your own experience of trying to live your life, over a long period of time,[2] partly by cross-examining the voices and the words that offer themselves for your inspection as bearers of the truth (here teachers and books are, of course, very useful, but they are not unexpendable, since teachers are to be found everywhere, in every walk of life,[3] at least as often outside the hallowed halls as

doxographical tables of "disjunctive truths" (a sort of *florilège des antinomies?*) into the poetry of the *Epistles;* he also seems to suggest that the "great" Arius Didymus, one of Augustus's teachers and very much in evidence at the court, supplied the doxographies in question. McGann, 17–19, 26–27, seems closer to the mark in trying to find a contemporary "influence" for Horace in Athenodrous Calvus, another of Augustus's entourage. Rawson, 255–57, has some dry and useful remarks on the nature of the philosophical enterprise at the imperial court which held true even in its early (Augustan) days.

[2] This view is very memorably captured in the words of Elstir (*A la recherche d'un temps perdu: A l'ombre des jeunes filles en fleurs,* ed. Pierre-Louis Rey [Paris: Gallimard, 1987], Collection Folio, 427): "*On ne reçoit pas la sagesse, il faut la découvrir soi-même après un trajet que personne ne peut faire pour nous, ne peut nous épargner, car elle est un point de vue sur les choses*" ("We're not handed wisdom; we have to find it for ourselves after a journey that no one can make for us or spare us from: because wisdom is one's own perspective on things as they are").

[3] Mayer, 1986, 67, emphasizes Homer (or poetry) as a moral guide espoused by Horace (*E.*2) as a replacement for, as superior to, formal philosophy; but the letter in question may be a not very affectionate parody of Stoic allegorizings of Homer (which, of course, used the poetry as a means to an end—we are back with Eliot and the poetry's not mattering; see p. 14 n. 5 above). More to the point would be Pollet's observation, 322: "Books are not pills that produce health in measured doses. Books do not shape character in any simple way—if, indeed, they do so at all—or the most literary would be the most virtuous instead of just the ordinary run of humanity with larger vocabularies."

within them, while "books" can also be thought of as the unwritten discourse of these informal teachers whom life supplies the learner with throughout his lifetime). In *E.*18, which is in some ways the climax of this book of letters, Horace tells Lollius how to go about looking for the true and the adequate. In *E.*2 he had offered him protreptic encouragement, but in 18, having found that the young man was apparently interested, really, only in making progress up the ladder of worldly (and wordy) success, Horace suddenly breaks off his instructions about *cultura potentis amici*—how to suck up to the rich and famous—and gives Lollius a few pithy hints about how to go about becoming a decent human being: "While you're learning to fawn and flatter and keep your master friendly and generous,"

> inter cuncta leges et percontabere doctos
> qua ratione queas traducere leniter aevum,
> num te semper inops agitet vexetque cupido,
> num pavor et rerum mediocriter utilium spes,
> virtutem doctrina paret naturane donet.
>
> (96–100)

You must keep reading and keep interrogating the learned philosophers in order to find out how you may live your life serenely, to discover whether insatiable desire will always shake you and vex you, as fears and hopes of things that are irrelevant to your happiness also do, whether it is dogma that brings us virtue or nature herself.

Note *percontor:* "ask," "interrogate"—just like Socrates.[4] Except

---

[4] Mayer's "Socratic," 1986, 72, has the advantage of removing the images and feelings intertwined with the word "Socrates" from a primarily Platonic context and of shoving them into a decorously more random world—that of the sophists, whose colleague Socrates was, and that of the post-Socratics, most of whom, including Aristippus and the Cynics, claimed him as their sire: it is the unstable affability (it can turn rather nasty when *kairos* demands), the stubborn zest and energies, the comic autonomy, the skepticism that really wants answers (that is, it is not shallow cynicism parading itself

that what Socrates as quizzer specialized in was ironic defabrications of the edifices of pompous knowledge and abstruse theory, whereas here the effort seems to be the collection of bits and scraps of wisdom (or common sense) from which to build ourselves a makeshift (yet adequate) lean-to, something suited to our particular (perhaps idiosyncratic) needs, something to shelter us from life's roughest weather. In any case, we read what we can get our hands on (or all we can take), and we question the wise to learn—not so much what they have to teach (nature does the teaching) as what they may say that might lead us to discover what might suit our own special case (and what most probably would not suit it).

But, like some other correspondents in this book of letters, Lollius, with his insatiable need, his *inops cupido,* will never have time to find out whether it is doctrine or nature that provides us with virtue (the courage, strength, and integrity we need to live our average daily lives decently); if he did try to make this investigation, he'd learn that both doctrine and nature make virtue possible for us, in different ways, at different times. From doctrines (emphatic plural) we get something we can test against our experience (and then can test our experience against it); then, equipped with that refined experience, we can add to or subtract from what *we* mean by the word "virtue" (and this process has no end). This definition (or redefinition) of the word (which develops, changes) is one that we have fashioned from our readings, our questions, our own experience, and our (constant) reformulations of the configurations they make (no one's lexicon, obviously, is going to be identical with those of his neighbors, but—was this the lesson of Prodicus?—most lexicons will, much of the time, tend to show reasonable affinities with one an-

---

about in order to annoy and to attract notice) that mark the Socratic mode, both in the early and middle Plato and outside Plato, in the gossip and anecdotes about him, in the imitations, some of them delightful, of his "followers" (Diogenes, for instance, and Aristippus and Bion). Of all this Horace takes what he can and uses it for his masks. For Socrates as sophist see Rankin, 13–14, 147–60, 198–202.

other). Doctrine, then, is overrated by philosophers (and maybe a little underrated by ordinary people, who, in turn, may tend a bit to overrate what they call "nature," that is to say, "customs," whose origins and initial developments and diverse functions have disappeared from memory); but Stoics, who delight in theatrical exaggeration, go much farther and actually attempt to equate nature with their own doctrine. For all that, and for all the scrutiny by all the philosophers, nature remains herself: fertile and various, extravagant and uncontrollable and capricious and inscrutable—utterly beyond the powers of reason to comprehend or imagination to mirror. Doctrine there must be, since humans have no real weapon but their wits, which, with a view to economy of effort, design doctrines and systems as helps to them in their attempts to understand and to master their circumstances. But when doctrine ceases to be strictly ancillary to nature, nature becomes impaired. The question, then, whether it is doctrine or nature that gives us *virtus* is an ironic pin to puncture philosophical pretension, and a doctrine for all men (and women) and all seasons is a lazy illusion.

In the next letter, 19, to Maecenas, on a very different theme, the horrors of poetic politics and the proper use of literary models, it is self-reliance, not slavish imitation (that is, adherence to doctrine), that is required for making use of a poetic tradition, that is, for making it new by making it one's own: *qui sibi fidet / dux reget examen*, "He who trusts in himself will rule the hive," 22–23 (a nice poetic expropriation of the political metaphor for "trivial" artistic ends). Poets who can't trust their own abilities (*o imitatores, servum pecus*, 19) end up botching the job. If someone were to try to impersonate Cato by looking wild and grim and going around barefoot wearing a two-bit toga (12–14), would we suppose that he was recreating for us Cato's virtues and morals? No. Because *decipit exemplar vitiis imitabile* (17): the model that is imitable in its vices (but not in its virtues) deceives us, promises us a shortcut to success, to happiness, to decency.[5] But

[5] In discussing Cicero's four-person theory (*Off.* 1.107–21), Gill, 173, attempts to solve the we/me dialectic that is the heart of Horace's first

all models are treacherous, because, unless we have examined
them critically before we try to possess them to make sure that
we can possess them, that they are suited to us, we will take their
shadow for their substance. And if we do examine them critically
and find them adequate to our needs, even then we will not take

---

volume of letters by deciding that Cicero's theory of personality, which in
my view is definitely something Horace had rumbling about in his head as
he composed his letters, might be granted authentic ethical status (even
perhaps by the rigorous MacIntyre) because it has "a rather minimal con-
ception of individuality," one that avoids "the kind of individuality that is
incompatible with satisfactory moral theory." This bad sort of individuality
is promulgated by Nietzsche in particular, and Gill congratulates Trilling
for his scrutiny of the author of *The Gay Science,* whose version of individuality is found to be radically ill suited to "more universalizing moral theories" and to "conventional social standards" (see Trilling, 119–21, 156–59;
and Krupnick, 130–33, 159–72). Unlike as he is to Nietzsche in many ways,
Horace would not be satisfied with Gill's solution (which is essentially the
a-few-rotten-apples wisdom dear to the hearts of nuns, gym teachers, and
drill instructors): it is a very delicate business, drawing the line between
we/me, finding when there is, at the right (necessary) moment, too much
of the one or too little of the other. For the ancient texts that bear on the
problem, see Long and Sedley 1:404, 427–28. For an imaginative rethinking
of the problem of the relevant ancient texts, see Asmis, especially 224–28,
240–42. See also Breguet, 1962, passim. It is worth perhaps pointing out
that in *De officiis* 1.107 the second *natura,* the one that governs the second
persona and its individual temperament, its unique nexus of virtues and their
defects, of gifts and limitations, must also have some influence over the
making of the third and fourth *personae* (1.115), which relate, respectively,
to class and to career (*natura* in 110, then, refers forward to 115 as well as
back to 107). In Cicero's version of personality, then, three of the four masks
are merely personal, and only one is universal. This emphasis is more
emphatic and more "modern" than readers of the *De officiis* seem willing to
allow, and perhaps explains some of the book's enormous popularity and
influence until, say, the death of Jefferson. Important for this view of the
significance of individuality for society and self, important, too, for its
insistence on the fact of the variety of temperaments, is *De oratore* 3.25–26,
227. The classic counterstatement is Plato's terrifying closure to the fourth
book of *The Republic,* where, it turns out, though there are indeed as many
kinds of states as there are kinds of souls (*hosoi . . . tosoutoi . . . tropoi . . .
posoi? . . . pente,* 445C–D), there is only one, good, really real city/soul, the
rest apparently being evil forgeries or perversions or careless miscopies of
the single truth. So much for pluralism (or relativism, as its enemies insist

all of them; often we'll take only a small part, one that suits us (*convenit*).⁶

In the matter of Horatian decorum, then, it is idle to talk of subjectivity (or to apologize for idiosyncracy or even eccentricity): what is at issue here is each individual's unique version of reality, which will be defined by its own peculiar admixture of truth and error, one's own inimitable collage of perceptions and illusions, one's own partial and thereby inevitably distorted view of things as they are, one's own portion of *vraisemblance*—a partial portion and a fragmentary one, one shot through with mistakes, a very poor thing, but all one's own and all one has— and adequate. Adequate, if one keeps on working hard at refiguring it freshly, to the purposes and pleasures of one's own life and perhaps to those of one's *socii* (one's band-and-village fellows).

Lollius, of course, is very far from grasping this irreverent cartoon of the good life and of how to try to begin trying to live it; he wants only to travel up to that room at the top (of the heap). In the first letter to him (2), however, Horace had talked to him (to use the Stoic metaphor that Horace disassembles in the *Epistles*) as if it looked as if he were on his way, as if he were setting out on the journey to good identity—or, as Horace might put it, in his own idiom, as if he were about to start finding himself an adequate identity, a persona that was a proper fit for his own, Lollian self, for this unique blend of virtues and their defects that each person is and becomes. At 35ff., Horace had suggested that

on calling it). The Roman elegists, for several reasons, are fond of this concept; it is not just for the purposes of his ironic priamels that Propertius employs it (2.1.46, 3.9.20), and Ovid, naturally, loves to affirm it *and* to send it up. Schopenhauer has some wise things to say about it in volume 2, chapter 55, of *The World as Will and Representation*. Mill's third chapter of *On Liberty*, "Of Individuality as One of the Elements of Well-Being," is the heart of his book and of his priceless gift to the world (it is also the heart of Gertrude Himmelfarb's fascinating effort, in 1974, to rescue the Arnoldian cosmos from the book's wicked subversions in her introduction to its Penguin edition).

⁶On *vitiis imitabile,* see Macleod, 1977, 366–67. For *conveniet: E.*10.43 (see *S.*1.7.10, 2.4.71, 2.8.48).

Lollius begin to get a move on (*dimidium facti qui coepit habet. sapere aude! / incipe!* "Well begun is half done—dare to taste the truth and distinguish its sweet from its sour flavors—become wise—begin!" 40–41). And at the end, in a gentle coda, 67ff., he begs him to begin changing his life: *nunc adbibe puro / pectore verba, puer, nunc te melioribus offer*, "My boy, drink in these words with a pure heart, give yourself to better things, now while you still can." The new jar, he reminds him, will keep the scent of what's first poured into it. "But if you dawdle, or if you sprint on ahead, I neither linger about, waiting for others to catch up, nor do I try to overtake those who've passed me by" (*quodsi cessas aut strenuus anteis, / nec tardum opperior nec praecedentibus insto*).[7] Horace and Lollius are not competing with each other or with other human beings in some sort of race to glory. At *E.2.2.204f.*, he describes himself: *viribus, ingeniis, specie, virtute, loco, re, / extremi primorum, extremis usque priores*, "In strength, wit, looks, virtue, position, money, I'm last among the first but always first among the last." (That's humble enough and swaggering enough.) If we were, he tells the callow young man, competing with anyone, it would only be with ourselves, but even that way of putting it smacks too much of aggression and vainglory when what we're trying to imagine, to focus our hearts on, is lighter than a feather in a breeze. We're not racing against one another or against ourselves, we're not competing—we're learning how to float.

In the letter to Maecenas that precedes the protreptic to Lollius, Horace chides himself for being so slow in changing his own life (*sic mihi tarda fluunt ingrataque tempora*, 23): I've ended up trying to guide myself and console myself with these handbooks, these introductions to philosophy (*restat ut his ego me ipse regam solerque elementis*, 27). Still, anything's better than nothing: *est quadam prodire tenus, si non datur ultra*, "It's something to have got a little way, even if it isn't given to us to go farther," 32. Despite the urgency, then, that marks his admonitions to Lollius in the

---

[7] For *praecedentibus*, see Moles, 37, who characterizes Horace as "half of a *proficiens*."

following letter, Horace's apparent indifference to how fast the journey is completed or even to whether it's completed or not shows yet another sort of irreverent attitude to the venerable Stoic metaphor of the Pilgrimage to God.[8]

The *proficiens* knows something of his goal and something about how to get there, and this image of the seeker on his path glimmers ironically in the *Epistles,* but it can't be said to shape them or to frame them, as, for example, it truly haunts Seneca's letters to Lucilius; certainly it hasn't the informing power that it will, diversely, show in Augustine's *Confessions* or in Bunyan's triumphant perfection of the metaphor in its purity or, in its modern transformations, in Goethe's meditative explorations of it in *Wilhelm Meister's Apprenticeship* or in Dickens's ironic renditions of it in *Great Expectations* or in Fitzgerald's sad and sequined evocation of it in *The Great Gatsby* or, finally, in James's definitive revelations of its dialectics in his incomparable *Ambassadors.* In place of arduous journeying, Horace favors other metaphors for discovering who one is: snoozing in the sun after a swim and lunch, sitting out in the sun and not saying much about what it is one's looking at. Horace has no method, no system, no path; it isn't at all clear that he is going much of anywhere, at least not in space-time. If the metaphor of spiritual journey is present in these letters, it is so only in Horace's dry, self-twitting refurbishing of its Lucretian version: he goes up and down the peninsula searching, hectically and querulously and vainly, for physical (and mental and moral) health, or he scurries to and from Rome.

But it is the farm he starts from, and to which he returns. And what he does on the farm and what he does traveling from and back to it is to ponder the things that are going into these letters. At most, it is the moment of becoming a *proficiens* that Horace imagines in the letters to friends and acquaintances. But even that probably goes too far toward the conventional (essential) motifs of the metaphoric cluster of road-traveler-journey's end. He wants to lead a better life than he's been leading. But what

---

[8] See Gagliardi, 67, 69.

would a good life be for (what should we want to be free for)? He
can define it frequently in a negative fashion. It is never, never a
life that is centered on money (but *voluptates,* alas, both big and
small, are seldom very far from the center, so he's always in
trouble with various kinds of puritans). Not greed, of the financial sort, then; but once one has got that in one's head, one wants
after reading these poems for a while to say to Horace (as I think
not a few readers have said to him, almost as they want, on
occasion, to say to Socrates): "OK, smart-ass, so what *is* virtue?
You've told us ad nauseam what it isn't. Is it being a nice kind of
guy, never having to say you're sorry, helping your pals and
smashing your enemies? Could you stop messing around, stop
turning the dictionary to confetti? Could you maybe put it in a
sentence?" The smile we might get from Horace as our full reply
would be Socratic (in a Roman sort of way, that is, for it might be
accompanied by a theatrical, if not Neapolitan, shoulder shrug);
it would be charming, but it would not be entirely agreeable. He
is not, after all, teaching us how to paddle our way to paradise.
He is trying to get our attention, trying to help us focus our eyes
on the hard fact that we, like him, have certain problems that we
spend most of our waking hours trying to ignore. We mistake
symptoms for the causes—of our bondage. The enemy of freedom is the illusion of freedom. We must learn to say, "This is not
it, that is not it," more readily than we're accustomed to. Some
travelers (to regress, for the moment, to the Stoic metaphor) set
out too early, and in the wrong directions.

It goes without saying that for a *proficiens* who has become a
Horatian honeybee (or a Taoist, as well as a Parnassian, but-
terfly), whose only goal is the next flower or, at most, the next
after that, there can be no guide (*nullius addictus iurare in verba
magistri, E.1.14*) except intuition, which might seem to be, to a
careless glance, caprice. Or put another way, one that is as suitable to Aristotle as it is to Horace, what matters is decorum and
kairos. Here spontaneity is of the essence. *Decus,* what is fitting,
what suits, means what one should do in *these* circumstances, in
this configuration of things and contingencies and volitions in

this time and place. It is, of course, what one makes of the circumstances, how, as it were, one reads them, that matters—or that matters, usually, at least as much as the circumstances themselves. Some paragon of *gravitas,* some soi-disant Cato, happily restricted by his tight, heavy toga, his face a mask of rectitude and disapproval, can—such is the power of his obsessions—wander unawares into a bubbling festivity and instantly convert it into a graveyard: all that these wantons needed (he thinks, surveying his handiwork, the party in ruins) was a little serious-ness, a little decorum. In this false version of decorum, essence precedes actualities, and it seeks to redesign actualities in its own image.[9] In the Horatian (and the Aristotelian) version of de-corum things change with the changes that surround them, and one masters one's situation by—paradoxically—yielding to it. In place of the Stoic's somber, pompous progression toward and ascent into the higher radiance, Horace offers a sort of wry picaresque, with lots of slippings and slidings and naps and lunches, or a leisurely saunter through a strange, often funny maze that turns out to be our own minds and hearts. We almost seem, as in going through the fun house or the house of mirrors, to end back where we began (progress, regress, cycle). In a sense, we go every place in this version of the search by learning to go no place: "sitting in forgetfulness, doing by not doing."[10]

But if it is not a place we are trying to get to, what are we trying to get (if we are trying to get something), what are we trying to do, or be? Somehow we want to become virtuous, but what does that mean?

One begins, as he says in 1.1, by learning to do without stupidity, by forgetting folly in order, perhaps, to remember sanity or to be able to see it with clear eyes: *virtus est vitium fugere et sapientia prima / stultitia caruisse.* The next step, as it were, would be to learn that *virtus est medium vitiorum et utrimque reduc-*

[9] For the eccentric mean and the ironies of decorum in the *Ars,* par-ticularly with regard to its closure, see Johnson, 1974, 78–83; see also Frischer, 61–62, 67–68, 77, 84–85, 98. Very instructive here is *De oratore* 3.177, 210, 212.

[10] Graham, 92 ("forgetfulness"); 21 and 35 n. 85 ("doing nothing").

tum, "Virtue is midway between its opposing vices," 18.9.[11] That (elusive) virtue (delicately balanced at equal remove—but not always at equal removes—from the vices that define it), that balance, that justice, is what he seems to be speaking of, at the end of 18, in his short, great prayer: "Every time I regain my sense of health and well-being with a dip in the icy Digentia— what, my friend, do you think is my state of mind, what do you think I ask for?"

> sit mihi quod nunc est, etiam minus, et mihi vivam
> quod superest aevi, si quid superesse volunt di,
> sit bona librorum et provisae frugis in annum
> copia, neu fluitem dubiae spe pendulus horae.
> sed satis est orare Iovem qui ponit et aufert,
> det vitam, det opes: aequum mi animum ipse parabo.
>
> (107–12)

May I keep what I have, or get along with less, and may I live for myself what's left of my life, if heaven decides that any *is* left. May I have a decent supply of books and enough food for the year. And may I not swing there, dangling from my hopes and fears from every doubtful hour. But it's enough just to pray to the god who gives and who takes to grant me life and the means to sustain it—it's up to me to provide myself with a balanced spirit, a just soul, a decorous heart and mind.

To certain varieties of the pious this prayer's closing clause may sound rather arrogant (just as the prayer as a whole might

---

[11] Arist. *Eth. Nic.* 2.9. The discovery (or rather, the rediscoverings) of the mean is an ongoing process performed by individuals in specific circumstances (not the fixed culmination of universalized search whose methods have been prescribed by experts); the *hote men . . . hote d'* (the swerving must be sometimes to the too much and sometimes to the too little) needs more emphasis than it is often given; such an emphasis might remind us that the context in which the swerving takes place is, as the poetic meditation on the figure of Aristippus in the previous poem suggests, always governed by *to prepon,* what is decorous, what is suitable *in this situation* for this uniquely configured person. See Davis, 167.

strike them as selfish and greedy and manipulative: he wants to live for himself, he wants a year's provisions, not just a day's, and he wants to make sure he has an adequate library). But Horace is not boasting here that he is one of the *perfecti;* he only says that he will provide himself—in each new set of circumstances, at each moment, for he doesn't say this prayer once and once only—he means he will try to provide himself, as *kairos* and his own *natura* require or allow or suggest, with a balanced spirit, a dynamic balance of heart and soul. As for the world and its changes (as for the 10,000 things, as the Taoists put it), all of it he accepts *grata manu* (11.23), gratefully, a friend to himself, *mihi vivat.* (So, in other places: *quid te tibi reddat amicum,* "what makes you a friend to yourself," *E.*18.101; *amico animo, Odes* 4.7.20; *pauloque benignius ipsum / te tractare voles,* "if you want to treat yourself a little more generously," *E.*17.11–12; *non horam teque esse potes,* "you can't be alone with yourself for a minute," *S.*2.7.112.) These verses, to my mind, are the climax of the book and its core, the stillness searched for and discovered, from which new motion again issues. How did he come upon the stillness?[12]

Let's go back to that moment at the beginning of this poem where he told Lollius and us that virtue is the equilibrium between opposing defects or excesses (*est huic diversum vitio vitium*

---

[12] Gagliardi, 62, argues that *aequus animus, aequitas,* and *modus* have long been in the repertoire and that the teaching of the poet seems not to have changed in the *Epistles* from what it was earlier. I would argue that the words and the phrase in question have changed with the changed context. What Horace says at the end of 11 and, particularly, at the end of 18 takes on a resonance that it lacked (in this mouth) before it encountered the situation of discourse that the poet designs for the *Epistles* (maybe from his life, maybe from his imagination, most likely from both). In this sense, the end of the prayer marks the culmination of Horace's attempt to shape the idea of Horatian balance of heart and mind, but the volume itself reminds us that the search for that balance in our lives cannot have closure (except in death, but that, of course, is not a closure we can use). Sarsila, 111, 135, sees *aequus animus* in *E.*18 as equivalent to the Horatian *duplex virtus,* a sort of interdependence of courage and acceptance, and this is attractive (except that in this scheme the traditional Roman virtue is jingoistic as well as muscular).

prope maius, "There's a countervice to this one, and maybe a bigger one," 5). Lollius has just been told that being obsequious, though rotten, is perhaps just a little less rotten than being a taciturn, spoilsport bore (we have heard of this polarity before, in the preceding poem, to which we'll presently be turning). Then the poet insists that while chronic irascibility might try to pass itself off as virtue, and chronic kvetching as moral splendor, particularly when they can manage to contrast themselves with fawning garrulity and in the glare of that specious comparison be taken for what they are not (*dum volt libertas dici mera veraque virtus,* 8), virtue is somewhere toward the middle of this bipolar spectrum. In the paradigm offered here to Lollius, between the vice of strong (but fake) affection from the sycophant and the vice of an uncontrollable candor of criticism from the heartless truth-teller there stands genuine friendliness. Will Lollius have snickered as his eyes grazed these lines? Surely this is very old and virtually worthless news? The tiresome mean between its two (more interesting) extremes—the famous gilded mediocrity! What could be staler, duller, less pragmatically attractive than that?

But perhaps the Peripatetic rule of thumb for finding virtue's whereabouts is not so fatuous or so facile in Horace's hands (or in Aristotle's for that matter) as it may have come to seem in the mouth of its patriarchal exponents (Polonius, for instance, or scoutmasters, perhaps, or various politicians and corporate chairpersons, local, national, or international). Let's turn back a few pages to the poem before this one, whose central images show the familiar bipolarities of rival wickednesses of defect and excess and their midmost balance. Here, on the one hand, is Diogenes, who gives his name to both immaculate honesty and inexhaustible, brutal incivility and whose only concern is his precious independence—free to live in the gutter as he chooses, beholden to none for the scraps of garbage he manages to get for his supper or the filthy water he ostentatiously slurps down. At the other end of the spectrum there is a nameless creature, Diogenes' opposite number in every way, a spineless marvel of moral decadence so utterly dependent upon his luckless patron, so vociferous in expressing his needs and whims, so cranky and pestering, that he becomes more than a nuisance to the patron whose affection he is soon to lose (17.52–62). Where, precisely, the recipient of this letter, Scaeva (Lefty) fits into this pattern is uncertain, though it seems possible that the closing lines of the poem, after the resonant climax of the central section, which features the man who makes a real effort to find his unique equilibrium (*experiens vir,* 42), perhaps constitute a word to the wise—perhaps Scaeva is prone to whining and complaining as well as groveling (this would form a good contrast with the *liberrimus* Lollius, the very free, perhaps too free, spirit, the tactless yes-man, of the next poem). Be that as it may, here as in the next poem, the emphasis is on the balance, on the virtue between rival extremes: which moral balance is here incarnated by Aristippus, whom we encountered early in the first poem of the book and who, in this poem, comes as close to being a paradigm for behavior as anyone in the *Epistles,* that is to say, the person with whom Horace seems desirous of claiming *some* affinity.

But in what way is Aristippus better than Diogenes? Given Horace's temperamental bias in favor of what used, wrongly and rightly, to be called civility (though that bias may in fact be one he *aspires* to having, may be part of what he needs *to find* for his integration), his preference for the frank hedonist over the grouch with a megaphone is hardly surprising; but the reasons for this preference go deeper than temperamental orientation. Diogenes' jibe at Aristippus is "If Aristippus could learn to dine on turnip greens, he wouldn't mess around with princes" (*si pranderet holus patienter, regibus uti / nollet Aristippus,* 13–14). Well and good, since princes attract sycophants as garbage attracts flies. This statement shows a radical and admirable sense of autonomy, and Aristippus's rejoinder to it, at first blush, seems rather feeble: *si sciret regibus uti / fastidiret holus qui me notat,* "If he who rebukes me knew how to mingle with princes (properly), he'd come to despise his dreadful vegetables," 14–15. *uti* in Aristippus's comeback seems to mean what it means in Diogenes' slur: "mix with," "mingle with." But his next remark, in clarification of his rejoinder, makes one want to retranslate *uti: scurror ego ipse mihi,* "I play the fool for my own benefit." This dative of self-advantage recalls their counterparts, *aequum mi animum ipse parabo* and *quid te tibi reddat amicum,* both of them in the next poem, to Lollius. *scurror ego ipse mihi:* "I enact the role of constant dinner guest, of parasite with the boardinghouse reach—but for my own purposes, not for those of my hosts who think they are using me, inviting me, for their purposes. You play the fool for the public, for the herd—to make an impression, to make a name for yourself: Diogenes, the revivalist comedian with the envenomed, knife-sharp tongue; and in the process of entertaining them by censuring them violently and wittily, you become their creature, you become your audience's plaything. Whereas I remain master of my audience. So I ride on horseback and eat wonderful food while you plod through the gutter and pick up from the slop whatever various lowlifes take a fancy to fling to you. And then you have the effrontery to claim for yourself absolute autonomy!" (*fers te nullius egentem,* "You claim that you need no one," 22; "but *verum / dante minor,* you are lower than the people who toss you scraps," 21–22.)

The suppressed portion of this contrast is "I'm in fact superior to the kings whom I allow to shower things on me. I make use of [not mingle with, *uti*] the rich, whereas you are used by the poor: they want to feel superior to someone; they provide you with a bare subsistence; they laugh both at your crazy jeremiads against them and a world you can't live in or change *and* at your vanity in supposing yourself really free from and superior to that world. You, the *farceur* of the garbage dump and the dung heap! O wonderful liberty! O glorious independence! Whereas I—no, I'm not free, except paradoxically, when I admit my dependency, when I give up the ridiculous notion that I (or any human being) need no one, when I acknowledge what it is that such freedom as I have depends on—then, strange to say, I do become, temporarily, the master of my situation (whatever the glaring ap-

pearances to the contrary may suggest), and I shape things to my
design rather than allowing myself to be squashed to fit the shape
of my circumstances. I am free when I go with the flow, when I
suit my desires to the possible. I get what I like because I contrive
to like what I get. Which allows me to move freely up and down,
here and there, without worrying whether the next shift in things
will cause me discomfort by disappointing my expectations, by
failing to meet my 'standards,' by deviating from my notions—
what more serious philosophers call ideas—of the real, the good,
and the true. I take life as it comes, and that willingness to accept
things as they are and as they come provides me with a peculiar
and enormous freedom. Whereas you, with your rigid—you call
them universal—motives of what's proper and improper, right
and wrong, good and bad, are constantly forced to reject most of
what you encounter in life. Your famous crust of bread, like the
stinking tub you live in, is in fact a symbol of that elaborate
defense mechanism of yours that protects you from the realities
you claim to confront head on and to conquer, but which in fact
you hide from—behind that shield of bad manners and filthy hair
and slakeless contempt for (or should I say, fear of?) existence.
You are no better than the soft, fat parasites whom you revile—
and mistake me for. But, in fact, I'm far better than either of you,
for I don't make myself miserable by seeking out and reveling in
the most degrading, bestial way of living in order to escape from
imaginary, or minor, humiliations and oppressions. And I don't
fool myself into pretending that I can outwit destiny or reality by
controlling things each moment or by forever reinventing the
world according to my abstract notions of what's good and
what's bad. On the other hand, I don't become so enamored of
fancy food and soft beds that I can't pull up stakes at a moment's
notice, then step out into the mean streets and get knocked about
in the traffic until fortune's next swerve sends me somewhere
cosier for a while. But both of you—the rabid puritan and the
delicate hog, twins in spirit, dead ringers under the skin—both
of you are locked into, frozen into, roles that will never change,
because you have let images of the good (contrary to each other

as they are) congeal your hearts, which should always be open, to the flux of things, to the rhythm of the world."[13]

Every shade and circumstance and situation of life suited Aristippus, who, though he aimed at the higher, was usually satisfied with what he had: *omnis Aristippum decuit color et status et res, / temptatem maiora, fere praesentibus aequum,* 23–24. There are those two small (big) Horatian words: *decuit, aequum.* Decorum and balance Horatian, *not* neoclassical, style. What suits *praesentibus,* the present (eternal) moment, things as they are, the actualities, here and now in front of us, here and now within us. There can be no perfect (foolproof) rule such as both the fretful parasite who closes this poem or such as the sour Diogenes, each in his different way, has made for himself and on which he has based his life—which he fails to live because he lives it immersed in a powerful illusion about the nature of what goodness is. What suits, what is proper, decorum, is iridescent, is a reflection of the 10,000 things in their changes, in their shifting configurations. Diogenes will not put on any garment that is not threadbare, for his tailor is Masochism (though the label reads Fortitude), and a change of scene, or of fortune even, will do nothing for him, because he is cemented into a misery that he claims is splendid (*mirabor, vitae via si conversa decebit,* "I'd be flabbergasted if he

---

[13] Moles makes a good case for Aristippus as a figure of "potential mediation between Stoic-Cynic and Epicurean poles," 38, but for him to function in this way, he needs to undergo a transformation by means of Panaetian moral "relativism," 45–49. A moderate, Stoical Aristippus might seem rather a droll confabulation, but Cicero's Panaetius has made his contribution to Horace's peculiar mediator; see Asmis, 240–42. And so, probably, has Aristotle, maybe by way of Panaetius. It is Aristotle (*Eth. Nic.*2, 5 and passim) who insists on the primacy of context and decorum. Perhaps it would be better to talk here of perspectivism (see *meson de ou to tou pragmatos, alla to pros hēmas,* 2.6.8) than relativism with its unfortunate connotations of Nietzsche bashing by neocons. See Courbaud, 250–52, who minimizes the value of Aristippus here by according him only a faute de mieux victory over Diogenes. For a possible parallel for Aristippus's paradoxical, unfree freedom, see "roam free inside the cage," Graham, 13, 69.

could benefit from a complete turnabout in his life," 26). Here is
decet again, now with a new irony, since nothing can truly suit
this grim caricature of humanity. As for Aristippus himself, he
has no need of a purple cloak to go out and be with other people:
*quidlibet indutus celeberrima per loca vadet, / personamque feret non
inconcinnus utramque,* "He'll throw on anything he happens to
grab and rush out into the crowded streets, looking rich or
looking poor, stylish either way," 27–28. Either mask will do
(the snazzy one, the down-at-the-heels one), since being at home
in one's skin is always in style—to those who know style when
they see it. Diogenes would rather go naked and catch pneu-
monia than wear something that wasn't in tatters. Then let him.
Let the poor idiot's teeth chatter in the chill wind.

As for Aristippus: surely Diogenes, not to mention Cato,
would find this business of wearing two masks alternately (or if
need be, almost simultaneously), of playing two parts (or more),
to be total proof of complete hypocrisy. But they would, in
making this judgment, be wrong. The capacity to shift, to take
up and lay down a public persona *pros kairon,* at the proper
moment, as decorum requires, is a sign of versatility, of course,
but it is also a sign of tolerance, acceptance of reality, common
sense, even of humility. With this new image of Aristippus in our
minds, one in which he is now an attractive, a possible, model of
identity, the poem's contrary vices and their relatively midmost
virtue look a little different than they did before the epiphany of
Aristippus. At the one extreme, spineless dependency, impo-
tence of will, stupid whim; at the other extreme, fanatic, obsessive, and fake autonomy, the steel will to pure selfhood, the
prisoner of its own delusions: poised between these wretched
polar varieties of defect and excess (each of them at once too little
and too much), the poem's reader can look back at the early lines
of the first letter to Maecenas, where, having claimed that he was
sometimes possessed of a Stoic's public-spiritedness (*nunc agilis
fio et mersor civilibus unda, / virtutis verae custos rigidusque satelles,*
1.16–17), the sly poet, congenital hedonist, incarnation (from the
puritan or Stoic point of view) of decadence and failure of nerve

and weakness of character, brazenly confesses his habitual infidelities to philosophical absolutes and Stoic disciplines: *nunc in Aristippi furtim praecepta relabor / et mihi res non me rebus subiungere conor,* "But now I slide back into the doctrines, as it were, of Aristippus, and I try to fit reality to my shape, instead of fitting myself to its shape," 18–19.

Relapse, recidivism, the Stoic's worst nightmare. That's how we may read it when we start the letters; however ironic the tone may seem here (the naughty boy cheerfully admitting his naughtiness), the poet's confession that, when wallowing in the hedonist mode, he tries reinventing reality to suit himself can seem only to indicate his recognition that the *praecepta* of Aristippus are invalid or harmful or both (and that, by implication, the dogmas of the Stoics are correct). But in 17, almost at the book's end, these lines take on a new sense. Being like Aristippus, backsliding again into this Latin version of *wu wei* (doing by not doing), of moving as the rhythm moves, going with the flow, taking the cookie as it crumbles—this is the preferred Horatian attitude. This renunciation of the Stoic version of obedience escapes the trap of pretending to know *vera virtus* and of trying to deform one's own life and the lives of others in order to make them fit some illusory (and dogmatic) notion of what nature is and wants, some abstract idealization of real life where a part of the truth is accorded universal applicability and a frozen, false, partial version of the truth(s) is allowed to construct its procrustean beds as it likes.[14] It is the Stoics and other fanatics, with their fatal cures for misdiagnosed sicknesses, who try to remake the world in the image of their deformed desire, and their cry as they do this and try to compel others to ape them is always *naturam sequor!* "I follow nature!"

[14] See Pelikan, 264, on Palamas: "He found the secret of orthodoxy in the fathers to be their capacity 'to observe both' aspects of a truth that was dialectical. . . . Heresy . . . consisted not so much in an outright denial of an orthodox dogma as in the adherence to one pole of a dialectical dogma at the expense of the other pole belonging to that same dogma." See also Hirschman, 88, 103–9.

Aristippus, on the other hand, may *say* (he is, after all, Socrates' most direct heir and thus well equipped as an ironist) that he is interested only in pleasure and that he forces things (nature) to adapt themselves to his need (*et mihi res*), but since what he wants is balance, a happiness that may include pleasure sometimes or often but that is in fact beyond pleasure, as it is beyond pain, it is he, paradoxically, the one who appears to specialize in arrogant and selfish manipulations of the world around him, it is he who truly shapes himself to the shifts of reality as decorum bids him to do. It is the good, wise, chameleon Cyrenaic who gives the lie to the real deformers of nature, those implacable reformers of the world who, with their unpersuadable, fraudulent dogmas, graciously allow the damned to witness their stately, steady progress, their grand and godly ascent, into the realms of perfection.

Having completed his sketch of Aristippus, Horace somersaults, in that outrageous way of his, from the contrast between the good chameleon and the miserable puritan to a discussion of the hierarchy of success. The opening contrast had turned on the question of how to win and influence the great. The question now is, What is the meaning, the value, of "getting to the top"? Wretched Diogenes, with *his* version of success, has now sunk out of combat into the slime, and one needn't worry about him and his tiresome moralizing and sourgrapery any longer. But the question remains, even after Diogenes has been silenced: Is all the effort one's put into getting ahead really worth it? King of the mountain, top of the heap—that position is reserved, of course, for the great princes of the world: *res gerere et captos ostendere civibus hostis / attingit solium Iovis et caelestia temptat,* "To triumph in battle and put the conquered foe on display is to touch with one's fingertips the throne of Jove, it is to essay the sky," 33–34. No trouble guessing who this is—who but *ipsissimus* himself, whose current incarnation is Augustus? So, if one can't be him, why make any effort to be anything? Because *principibus placuisse viris non ultima laus est,* "To have found favor with the chief men is hardly to have snatched the least glory," 35. Then, what I take to be rather bad news, *non cuivis homini contingit adire Corinthum,* "Not everyone can live on the Upper East Side—and afford to live there; not everyone gets to be a big shot and attain real glory," 36. This *is* bad news for Scaeva, whose value system frames the surface of this poem and to whom its surface arguments are addressed. And since the probabilities for big success aren't all that hot, mightn't Scaeva reply: "Why bother, then— why go to all the trouble of groveling and fawning if the return isn't in six, that is, seven figures with various perks and a golden parachute tossed in?" To this implicit question cum complaint, Horace points out: *sedit qui timuit ne non succederet,* "He who was afraid he wouldn't win just sat there in the bleachers, you lose every race you fail to enter. Nothing ventured, nothing gained, etc.," 37.

I'm fairly sure Scaeva tossed the letter aside at this point in his scanning it for useful info (call him here the fictive, ideal, initial, intended reader). If later on he happened to pick it up, he found, around 43ff., some advice, as ironic in this context as it is realistic and efficacious in what we charitably call the real world, some advice that he might have put to good use as he smirked and clawed his way up the infamous, unglamorous ladder to small successes. For all that, my sense is that Horace is not all that unfond of Scaeva. As compared with Lollius, who is full of all manner of rationalizations and excuses for his maneuvering up the ladder and captivating the rich and famous, Scaeva seems refreshingly candid about his needs and greeds—which is why the advice he would have found had he finished reading the letter was potentially valuable to him: Don't be such a whiner, smile and keep your mouth shut, and you'll get more and get on better than you've recently been doing in your chosen profession, that of yes-man.

But enough of Scaeva, who, though he and his ineptitudes as *scurra* close the poem in a formal way, drops from its center just where we left him, formally, a moment ago: You can't win if you're scared of losing. So be it: *esto.* Then: *quid qui pervenit, feciatne viriliter?* 38. H. R. Fairclough, in his Loeb version, renders this thus: "What of him who reached the goal? Did he play the man?" *atqui / hic est aut nusquam quem quaerimus,* "Hey now, here or nowhere is exactly the guy we're looking for!" 39. *pervenit* as "reached the goal" certainly suits the *proficiens* motif, but there are other sorts of "finishes," and the word can mean "to go as far as one can," and so, "to be finished," "to die." This seems to be the connotation that the context in the rest of this passage requires. *hic onus horret / ut parvis animis et parvo corpore mauis,* "One person is afraid of the burden (of life, of not trying to win the rat race) on the grounds that it's bigger than his small body and small spirit can deal with," 39–40. *hic subit et perfert,* "But somebody else (our kinda guy) just picks up his load and trudges off with it and keeps on carrying it until he drops." *aut virtus nomen inane est, / aut decus et pretium recte petit experiens vir,* 41–42: either *virtus* (acting like and being a man, *viriliter*—no way to mask these phallocentricisms) is just a word (a lot of crap) or the person who makes an effort to live his life well, rightly (*recte,* as in 42 or as in *rex erit qui recte faciet;* see above pp. 41–42), aims for honor and reward (*decus et pretium*). Yes, but *decus* (cognate with *decorum*) and *pretium,* though they fix themselves easily and neatly into the surface meaning that Scaeva and Augustus and the great world attach to them, also mean—and Horace here does one of his back flips—the distinction and dignity and recompense, the balance and serenity, that are the reward of the man whose eye is fixed on true happiness, on *kairos* and *aequus animus.* At his journey's end the *proficiens* will perhaps take possession of a (relatively) enduring residence in one of those stars that Cicero spoke so eloquently of in the *Somnium Scipionis* and made so central to the culture of the West in its Latinate phases: he will enjoy both historical and astronomical memorials to a life well lived on his road to glory. Aristippus, on the other hand, the *experiens vir,* the man who does his damndest, who tries hard to seek true rewards truly, that is to say, decorously—he belongs to a different breed. No one will see how he strains *not* to do great things, but rather to live a decent life. In a sense he will not know this himself, because he will be too busy living his life to notice how he does it. Furthermore, it is not the goal that matters any longer, since mere destination exists in the (unreal) future and that means the *experiens,* rather than dreaming of some life he hasn't, is trying to live the life he has, not according to prescription but by "forgetting what he usually remembers in order to remember what he usually forgets."[15] The *experiens* enjoys the journey, the day to dayness of it, the minute to minuteness of it (as Cavafy's grand poem "Ithaka" recalls for us). Regarding neither past nor future, he is not merely existing, passing through the world (any more than he is sacrificing himself and those around him to the past or the future), but he is, by virtue of his clear regard for what is around him and in him, actually living in the world, richly, passionately, and serenely. It is the going that matters, not the goal. It is the plenitude of our living and our glad, grateful consciousness of the world we do that living in, not some specious perfection of it, that counts. Diogenes Laertius tells us that when someone rebuked him for cohabiting with the famous Lais, Aristippus replied: *ekhō, all'ouk ekhomai—epei to kratein kai mē ēttasthai hēdonōn ariston—ou to mē khrēsthai,* "I have her, she doesn't have me. The best way to live is to be master of one's pleasures rather than their slave—but to renounce pleasure out of fear is hardly the right way to live," 2.75. ("Madam," said Dr. Johnson to the abbess, "you are not here for the love of virtue, but from the fear of vice.") Neither too much nor too little. Choosing enough at the right time, in the right place, as one's instinct bids one—that is decorum, that is selecting from the spectrum of values and actions the difficult, elusive, midmost virtue.

Horace had learned from the practice of his art, and most particularly from the composition of the poems that make up his first collection of lyrics, what striving for perfection was, what it entailed. But that knowledge, its habits of choosing and rejecting, its ordering of priorities, its mediations between vitality and

[15] But see Moles's interesting argument, 45 and n. 70: *experiens* as a subversion of Cynic terminology.

order, he could not transfer to the new crises of his life. Artists are ordinary people with extraordinary burdens and extraordinary gifts. In the matter of living their lives they are no better prepared than the rest of us—indeed, because of the nature of their gifts and the ways in which they need to husband those gifts, they are not infrequently much less prepared—for living their lives in ways that satisfy them, as against making art in ways that might someday satisfy them. So Horace learned, was learning, a commonplace sort of humility. If he had come to fancy himself as a *proficiens* at some time in the past, before various crises converged and led to the poetic incubation that led to the composition of the *Epistles,* by the time he came to write these poems, or at some time during the gestation of their *donnée,* he had come to see that he was, aside from his poetic gifts, no different from other humans, that the artistic greatness that he had striven for so fiercely and had in fact obtained was not going to be, could not be, matched by a complementary or equivalent moral or spiritual greatness, that like other people he had to find his own balance, make his own peace with life and resentments and mortality, honestly and humbly.

The new *askēsis* (let's call it learning to pray after a dip in the chill stream, after a picnic lunch and a snooze in the sun), was intended to replace a seemingly defunct artistic (that is, lyric) *askēsis,* but as it was gropingly gathered, and put together piecemeal, through trial and error, it turned out to be no less artistic, in a new way, than it was moral. Summoned into existence to counter caprice and pain and loss (and the chaos of his volatile, now impotent gifts, and the welter of poetic experiences that fed the gifts, and the resentments and sufferings that fed the experiences), in the event, instead of diminishing instability or exorcising anxiety, the new *askēsis* found itself being countervailed by caprice and desire and muffled memories of old angers, found itself being balanced by what it balanced, by what turned out to remedy its own defects. Too much caprice, too much feeling? Yes, but—also too much askēsis, too much dry pondering.

He did not then, retire, after all, to the farm for good. That would not bring balance, would offend the decorum. There were not infrequent (and probably mostly rather pleasant) trips back to Rome—to see his friends, even to train the chorus for the funny hymn. If he stayed in the country and made it a rule never to return to the bustle and tumult and to his friends, he would risk becoming something of a freak, he would have no interest but himself and his spiritual progress (as they called it), a cartoon sage in his narcissistic cartoon refuge, furiously at work on his dreadful treadmill to *aretē*. So he would leave the pure inwardness to others. It takes all kinds (*esto aliis alios rebus studiisque teneri, E.*1.81), but being a hermit or being a hermit purely was not his style.

For all that, there was something specially his own about the farm. He seems not to be touched by any sort of agnostic mysticism—something vaguely akin perhaps to what we find in the Taoist masters—yet one wants to qualify that denial slightly.[16] Even in *S.*1.6.60, *o rus quando ego te aspiciam,* there is already that somewhat ironic, bemused tug toward country calm that is so frequent in the lyric poems and that haunts the *Epistles* and becomes incandescent at the beginning of *E.*1.16. Yet even there, where beauty is allowed a rare, explicit intrusion, the final emphasis is on utility, the health that the countryside proffers: *hae latebrae dulces, etiam, si credis, amoenae, / incolumen tibi me praestant Septembribus horis,* "This refuge of mine, so delightful, yes, I'd even say, so lovely, keeps me in health even in the heat of September," 15–16. But perhaps this is slightly ironic, this dull Roman emphasis on utility versus loveliness. There is something else in this gaze out at the world of nature, something beyond both the *utile* and the *dulce.* An intuition of *concordia discors* defines a part of that gaze, but beauty, or something beauty stands for (not as in Sappho, of course, though Sappho was certainly in his blood), focuses it even more sharply. Horace does not, in the high Romantic fashion, look steadily into the beauty to see

[16] See Rudd, 1966, 241–43, for a sketch of how a "strict agnostic" attempts to deal with the unearthly happiness the country affords him.

what's beneath it. His style of seeing is other. Think of Soracte or
Bandusia or the Digentia. It is the briefest glimpse, a glance
maybe over his shoulder, from the corner of his eye. But what he
sees, those moments of the look of the countryside, are as vivid
and unforgettable as they are momentary. And these pictures of
the world of nature, together with the dialectical struggle revealed in *Epistles* 10–19, hint to us the shape of the images of
freedom(s) he was looking for, for himself, for us. Those pictures of serenity are the product of an immense turbulence,
outside him and inside him, and they are discreet, apophatic,
imprescriptive.[17]

[17] Anderson, 51, notes "a graceful resignation to age" that sharply contrasts with the Yeatsian wild old man; Armstrong, 122, 133, 155, speaking
of the "life-review" Horace performs in the later poetry, discovers a pattern of harmonious convergence and completion (in *E.*1.18, 133, and in
*C.*4.137) that smacks not a little of Pound's posturing Herakles: "Splendor!
It all coheres!" Kenney, 238–39, defines the wit of *E.*15 brilliantly and shows
how the poem subverts the picture of the *proficiens* "that had seemed to
emerge from *E.*10 onwards." But this correct emphasis on the poet's self-
irony ignores the pattern of more varied and complicated ironies that
inform 16–18 (whose "serious" facets Armstrong, 127–33, sees clearly). For
the permanence of the discontent, which entails the permanence of effort to
overcome it, see Gagliardi, 73–74. For a subtle formulation of the ficticity
of this integration, see Hirt, 312–29. For the inevitability of the topos of
integration in the genre of autobiography, see Olney, 41–42, 48, 140–47,
321.

[5]

THE PERMANENCE
OF CHANGE

The more the subject fancies itself to exist, and to be, in its own
eyes, an unsponsored entity, the less a subject in fact it is.
—Theodor Adorno

The question of the form (*Gehalt*) of the *Epistles* (or, to put it in
a slightly different way, of their genre) is a vexed one, and is
likely to remain vexed. Few readers seem now to believe that
these are real letters that were really sent and that really expressed
the sorts of thoughts, emotions, and opinions that real (and
ordinary) epistlers express when they write letters. But if we are
fairly certain that real letters are not in question here, and feel
therefore free to go on to investigate other, more plausible generic kinships for the *Epistles,* does it necessarily follow that
real letters were not a part of Horace's inspiration for what seems
his original creation—this factual-fictive missive, this hybrid of
what-might-be (*hoia ta genomena*) and of the fiction of correspondence, of the spiritual autobiographical in imaginary letters?
Horace may dimly have had either Epicurus or Cicero or both at
the far back of his mind at some early stage in the predevelop-
ment of the form that his new hexameter book would eventually

take, but suppose the story of its inception goes more like this.[1] Suppose one day he was dictating a letter to Maecenas (or, more likely perhaps, to Bullatius or Torquatus or Fuscus), some letter to a close friend (not to an acquaintance, to some lowly or highly inmate of the hive). He is really working at this letter, really saying what he means and feels—and then, suddenly, something flashes into his mind, and he is almost reminded of something that he can't quite get hold of. Not until late that night or at some random moment the next day does he begin to realize that something in the tone of the letter somehow reminds him of the *Satires,* something in the *Satires.* . . . Something in *E*.6, say, where he is talking about himself in order to say something about life as most of us live it (what he really has almost remembered maybe is the voice of Davus, the slave, saying things about him he carefully doesn't know). So, though he hardly feels like writing satires any longer (because, for instance, he is tired of criticizing people; the satirist is running on empty), though he has given up satire, he still likes his prosy hexameter style, and he likes those old poems of Lucilius (despite and because of their awkward cadences), which, so far as we know (which isn't very far), were, some of them, little self-caricatures, fragments of personal reminiscence about self—not autobiography in the usual sense, but a self using the self as a symbol, an image, of all lives. That form—and the style of writing that goes with it—has a nice ease about it; it is deceptively casual, it is persuasive, one can pack a

[1] See Williams's discussion, 519–21, of the importance of Cicero's model here; for the possibility of Menippean satire as model, see Dilke, 1844. Malherbe, 1988, provides a useful collection of ancient observations on the genre of epistles, its styles, functions, and kinds: Pseudo-Demetrius, 31, counted twenty-five kinds and suspected that time would uncover more; Pseudo-Libanius, 67–73, proved him to have been correct by bringing the total to forty-five, the last of which, the mixed, seems, unsurprisingly, to be the Horatian favorite. For the letter as autobiography, see Gusdorf, 152–55. Dowling's discussions, 11–14, 29–31, 37–38, 91–93, 176, and passim, found themselves on a complicated and unlikely view of the *kairos* of the genre: reasonable and attractive in theory, in application messy and intractable.

lot into those anecdotes—and one can observe human behavior and the passing show without carping too much at the big bad world and its tawdry utopias, and one can twit oneself (which god knows one needs and deserves) dryly, amusingly, without maudlin self-flagellations. And some of what one says will stick in the mind, the more so for being so transparent, so light. "But better than talking about myself directly to my reader or to some fictive interlocutor, in some conventional *mise-en-scène,* suppose I use, as I do in the lyrics, an intermediary? So I write letters to friends or acquaintances which the reader is, so to speak, allowed to intercept—as if he'd found them, their seals broken, lying in the street. Why shouldn't he—though it's wicked to read some-one else's mail—read these? In this way I can talk about myself without the pompous monumentality that kings and statesmen fall into when they're discoursing on what they've done and who they are, and I can also evade the didacticism, the grim avun-cularity, that philosophers automatically adopt when, under the guise of furnishing friendly advice in a letter to a disciple, they repeat, in only a slightly different way and in a slightly more colloquial style their usual prescriptions and proscriptions and ipse dixits. What I can do is invent a correspondent, Horace, who will remind my readers of the old satirist they're used to, dif-ferent though he is—a little older, a shade wiser, a touch less testy. Hence the pleasures of novelty neatly blended with the pleasures of familiarity."

That might have been what part of the rational part of Horace's mind came upon. But other, less rational, or at least less con-scious, parts of the mind were saying something else: "Yes, and we will get to talk about the Name of the Father and Desire and the Other and discords that aren't so very concordant after all, little man. We'll get to explain what happens when the mirror cracks, and we'll get to talk a lot about how we don't want to die and how success is a huge boring lie. We'll get to apprise your patient listeners about bondage and surfeit, about how frighten-ing it feels to be free when one was almost born a slave, when one could have been a slave, of how guilty and anxious one feels, or how weird it is for one to be born free and another to be born a slave. Oh yes, we'll have plenty to say while our lucid, prudent, intellectual poet, secure in his cheerful, benign mask, croons his humanistical drivel to himself and his dupes—and while he sings them lullabies we'll have for them a delicious undersong—we'll be screaming to our heart's content, mad as the mist and snow." The darker—or as they would term themselves, the more genuine—selves were happy to cast their vote for the new generic experiment, knowing as they did that without them there would, of course, be no poems worthy of the name.

One advantage of the letter over the satire was its increase in civility and in range of tone. His uniform satiric laughter, whether slightly shrill or much muffled, as was needed, had been all right in its proper places, but satire, which fitted his talents so well, could not lend itself easily to the softer feelings that advancing age and his new situation brought with them. In talking with his readers as if he were talking in letters to friends he could modulate into the softer style when and as he pleased (just as he would when dictating real letters); on the other hand, if he wanted the older style or something like it, he could present himself writing to someone who was something less than a friend, a Scaeva, a Lollius, or he could write to Augustus or Tiberius, and, with deft shading, a little rancor could find its way into the new, larger, more civilized form. What he did not want now, now or ever again, was to stand up on his Cynic soapbox and effuse cavils and rebukes. His energies were less forthcoming than they'd been, and his peeves had dwindled somewhat—it was time for younger and sillier men to preach to their betters (or their elders).

Still another advantage to the verse epistle: in the lyric books he had grown used to shaping poems that were intended to be further shaped in the complex reciprocities of their complex configurations into ever larger, more lucid, and more iridescent shapes as readers experienced them, as they performed them, as it were, in their minds and hearts when reading them or, as was more likely the case, hearing them read. Satire, on the other hand, was more of a grab bag. Even though one arranged these poems in an exquisite order, people tended not to notice the exact designs, because what they expected was a crowded buffet, and that's the way they tended to treat a satiric collection, loading up on this, skipping that, skimming, chuckling, returning to where they found their chief guffaws, ignoring "the echoes and the mirrors." But verse letters, though they represented moments, episodes, though they were fragments of living, were, by their very nature, possessed of a unity that could not be avoided. In addition to the unity of themes and that of the epistler persona— the speaking-writing voice(s)—there was the grand unity of the correspondents, the circle of recipients. For the letter itself was a perfect symbol, a unifying symbol, of much that he wanted to say: about speech and communication (and their failures as well as their triumphs), about civility, their reciprocity, persuasion, about ties that bind and the need (which Epicurus had seen so well) for friends, for the solace of friendship.[2] Here, perhaps, the poet's Superid and its offspring, bored to tears in their dark cellar by all this humanistic maundering, began to howl: "Yes, and you get to complain to them, too, don't you? You get to tell them all your troubles, how miserable and misunderstood you are, and you get to tell them what idiots they are. If you love your precious friends so much, why do you do anything to get away from them, down here in the middle of nowhere on your fake farm?" But if he heard those nasty, dim voices, he ignored them, and he concentrated on the more civil and civilizing reasons for choosing, for reinventing, the epistle form, and he began to write verse letters that were about himself and his world to people who either represented and were part of the world he loved and was most at home in or who, on the contrary, represented what seemed to him most alien to that world and most threatening to it.[3]

[2] See Perret, 112–14; and Kilpatrick, 106–9.

[3] See Hirt for a somewhat similar, rather more transcendental version of the rhetorical dynamic of writer/reader/letter/message/response, in particular, 68–72, 197–98. This is an original and powerful reading of the idea

Such seem to be the possible reasons, or rather causes, for the birth of this Horatian epistolary genre. But even if these speculations were correct, some questions would remain. If the unity and verisimilitude (which letters offered him so abundantly) were so important in this choice (or this invention) of genre, why didn't he enhance this gain by providing a vivid or at least a plausible sequence for the letters? To have given fictive letters fictive dates might not have occurred to him (much as the convention seems "natural" to us), but why not bother to shape some sort of narrative pattern for them? One of his big themes after all is that of the *progrediens*. He has left Rome and lyric (and maybe all) poetry behind him in order to make some progress in his moral life. Why shouldn't he pay some attention, in and through the ordering of the letters, to the articulation of that progress? As a matter of fact, if one of the book's major themes is change, conversion, development, don't the poems (the letters) *require* an imitation of progress, or, to defuse the metaphor a little, of changes in his spiritual condition, of the moments of conflict from which some of the hard-won harmony at last emerges? Why forgo the distinct mimetic advantage of a fictive sequence, one that the genre would seem to suggest and indeed seem almost to demand? One thinks here of the gorgeous parody of this aspect of the genre's "essential" pattern in *The Screwtape Letters*. Closer to Horace in time and maybe in spirit, of course, is Seneca, who makes much of the *progrediens* topos (indeed, his version of the one who is one his way, who has started out, is, apart from Apuleius's, the most extensive we have in ancient Greek and Latin literature until Augustine's); Seneca does seem to start with a sort of sequence for the topos in his early letters to Lucilius, and one gets the sense that he thinks of his fictive

---

behind the poems, but it is, in addition to being repetitious and exhaustive in tracing the nuances of its central theses, so committed to the *symbolic* nature and function of these poems that it utterly misplaces the facts of the fictions that help create the illusion of reality—without which the poems are neither entertaining nor illuminating. For this style of imagining reception (and intention), see Holub, 66–67.

correspondent (and perhaps of himself) as in the process of progressing or at least as being truly capable of moral progress. For a while in his *Epistles* one seems to be watching the beginnings of progress as well as hearing, among many other things, about the nature and meaning of such progress. But, for whatever reason, even Seneca lets his natural, or easy, mimetic strategy slip away from him. After a while, our sense of the reality of Lucilius seems also to fade, and very soon after this, Seneca is busy contributing to the genre that Plutarch will perfect (the essay) and begins to pay only perfunctory attention to the most minimal of epistolary formulae. But if Seneca became increasingly careless with the formal features of the genre, the question is still, Why did Horace, with, for example, Cicero's clear example fresh before him, not try to see what chronology and narrative design could add to his meditation on the psychic conflicts and drama of a soul's struggles *with* change, a soul struggling *to* change? Crucial as these questions are, I leave them for a time and turn now to consideration of something that may help us to answer them, namely, the character or mask(s) of the epistler. Perhaps a description of the self that writes these letters will help us to see how it shapes the patterns of its actions and its observations.

In these premature postmodernist, post-Freudian (not to mention posthistorical) days of ours, to mention the self without a slow crimson suffusing our faces is surely not easy. But in looking over a book, say, like *The Book of the Self: Person, Pretext, and Process,* edited by Polly Young-Eisendrath and James A. Hall, where twenty-two psychiatrists and psychologists, including a few stray humanists, ponder what meaning(s) the word *self* could be said to have in our era, after getting some sense of the wide spectrum of ideologies and opinions and troubles the word summons into existence, I come to the conclusion that there seems to be nowadays no very clear agreement as to what the word may or may not mean, while lively debate appears to flourish as to whether the word means anything much at all—that is to say, as to whether there is or is not some entity to which the word might be said to refer. What I can piece together from several of the essays that seems useful to my look at Horace is the notion of a kind of core in the great mass and mess of feelings, impulses, illusory thoughts, self-hypnotic habits of seeing, velleities, and obsessions that we call, depending upon our class, gender, tribe, politics, and intellectual orientation, self or personality or soul or psyche, a kind of core to all that welter of experience which tries to use memory and language and expectation to tell itself (and others, but mostly itself) stories about itself and itself's experiences of the world, which it does to ward off the anxieties it feels about being and about being itself.[4] This core of self (if it exists) is or is the product of or the representative of a system of self (a self-system) that protects the self against real or imaginary dangers by distinguishing what is beneficial to the self from what is or is possibly harmful to it. (Before I proceed any further in my *bricolage* from this (and other books) let me admit that while thumbing through it and jotting in it I sometimes had the feeling that this was "déjà vu all over again," in a certain way: namely, some of this review of psychic structure and process seemed a little like consulting a Homeric lexicon for emotional and intellectual terms, with frequent forays into R. B. Onians when the chips were down; it would be hard to overestimate the sophistication of Homeric psychic diction and its elegant, precise indeterminacies.)

Suppose, then, there is a core to our psychic experience, to our selves, and that core is, so to speak, essentially a storyteller, not very different in its ambitions from Scheherazade. Unlike a computer, it makes very large and very frequent random errors, and it is in fact very much more wrong (but sometimes almost deliberately) than it is right.[5] To call it a core is, moreover, slightly misleading, since it is less a thing than a process: a process of separating what belongs to the self (decorum again) from what doesn't. And this process never ends (because, of course, the

[4] See Loevinger, 93.
[5] See Spence, 133.

tale's end, like its beginning, is not perceived). The teller of the tale never takes a vacation and never goes into retirement, and, as a matter of fact, it never even goes to sleep; while the rest of the self that is the teller's constant audience snores away in order to have the strength and focus to get the experience from which the tale can be patched together, our unwearying teller is busy telling more tales (and telling some of the most fascinating and significant ones as we sleep and apprehend them, usually, inadequately). But let me sum up this part of my description of the self with the completion of Paul Kugler's précis of Lacan's theory of the self:

> The realization that subjectivity is constructed leads to the awareness that we are *in* language and creating metaphors of ourselves, as well of our understanding of ourselves, all the time. Subjectivity is not given, nor are the myths we have of it. Subjectivity is something constructed continuously through metaphorizing in every dimension in our existence, including theory making, free associating, and every other dimension of representation that exists after the advent of language. Whether this constructing and metaphorizing activity exists before the psyche is constructed through language is impossible to say, but certainly it is an irreversible fact that we live in the world of language.[6]

Wortwelt: the wordworld, the word's world. If all this seems rather de trop (and remember, Lacan didn't, when he was in his prime, want our agreement or even our disagreement so much as he wanted to scare us into sanity), let's recall a soberer or at least a more tradition-sanctioned authority in this matter. "I didn't so much write my book," says Montaigne, "as my book wrote me (*mon livre m'a fait*)." When someone undertakes seriously to describe herself or himself (when I say "seriously," I do not have in mind just another creature from politics or show biz or big biz seeking to set the record straight), what seems to me to take place

---

[6] Kugler, 180–81; see also G. White, 352–57.

is the process that Georges Gusdorf means by his *découverte de soi*:[7] if one began by trying to show oneself in a certain light, to reveal something complete, finished, intelligible (think of Hellman's superb titles for her autobiographies—*Pentimento, An Unfinished Woman*), what one ends by doing is becoming something else, something new. In short, in trying to tell one's story one has in fact been rewriting one's story, that is to say, rewriting oneself. Nor is this something that only writers do, or public figures who become writers temporarily in order to tell their stories in a public and permanent manner ("to correct" the record).

We all do it, as Freud says, as Lacan says; as Freud, more than anyone discovered; as Lacan, in a way, rediscovered, brilliantly, when he saw that the heart of the matter is not so much pictures of the primal scene—which are in fact words about pictures—as it is the way our minds and memories are structured like language, almost by language, because he saw that language is what we live in and through as well as what we use to tell and retell and untell our various moments of initiation and transformation. We all do it—on planes and trains and buses, in waiting rooms or barber chairs or bars. We do it while our spouses or lovers are attempting to get some sleep. We do it when we are shaving or brushing our teeth or stirring the stew or trundling the shopping cart down a supermarket aisle. We do it especially perhaps on the phone, particularly in times of stress, but before phones were invented or before sly advertisers had fooled us into thinking that a phone call was somehow magically less expensive than a stamp, we used to do a great deal of it by letter (which is why we know what we know, by and large, about the lives and sensibilities of our nearly forgotten ancestors). And what we are doing with our telephones and what we used to do more frequently with pen and paper is/was precisely what Clarissa Harlowe did and what Ovid's admirable crazy ladies did, and what Horace, himself, fictively yet not entirely fictively, is doing:

[7] See Gusdorf, 31–32, 120–30.

We are all the time constructing narratives about our past and our future and that core of our identity is really a narrative thread that gives meaning to our life, provided—and this is a big if—the thread is never broken. Break the thread and you will see the opposite of the story. Talk to patients in a fugue state, to patients with Korsakoff's syndrome or Alzheimer's disease, and you will sense the terror that lies behind not knowing who you are, what happened yesterday, and what will happen tomorrow.[8]

Once the thread is broken. We need to tell our story. We want it to be a true story, of course, one that is faithful to what happened, but mostly we want it to be a significant story, to have meaning, so that our lived experience will have a coherent meaning. And unless we make a pattern of them, both the happenings we author and those we merely encounter tend often to seem fragmentary, to seem (in Donald Spence's words) "random," because without our patterning of them their contingency, their flux, and our sense of our not quite completely seeing them whole combine to make us anxious (about what really happened, about what may happen as a consequence, about who we really are . . .).

If contrasted with classical theories of personality (cartoons of Plato, for instance, with a stern if benevolent Superego efficiently keeping his ego and id friends in bondage), such a notion of self may seem too problematic, too obviously akin to our various cultural and metaphysical pessimisms that attempt to authenticate themselves with linguistic and epistemological credentials. But trendy and suspiciously too current though it may seem, this version of the self has, for the purposes of literary criticism, obvious attractions: it makes sense to the reader of literature to hear that identity originates in and is sustained

---

[8] Spence, 143. In this regard, the stories of Korsakoff's syndrome in Oliver Sacks's *The Man Who Mistook His Wife for a Hat* have extraordinary resonances.

and illumined by language and narrative; that the self is a self-constructing artifact that uses narrative to achieve its essential purpose, which is to keep rewriting itself as long as it needs to, that is to say, as long as it has life.

One thing that has happened in this version of self which has importance for my attempt to read Horace is that all idea of self-knowledge has been replaced by self-representation, which is hardly the same thing as self-knowledge.[9] Recall, too, that one of the great masters of *autoanagnorisis,* the industrious and indefatigable Montaigne, summarily rejects the famous Delphic inscription that also attracted the irony of Socrates: "C'éstait un commandement paradoxe que nous faisait anciennement ce dieu à Delphes" (3.9, De la vanité). A paradoxical command. Look into yourself, know yourself. Can one in fact know the self? Who, except Socrates himself, is better able to answer this question than Montaigne? Yet it is he who reminds us that it is when we are miserable that we are most introspective (3.9). And if that were not obstacle enough to self-knowing, he reminds us also (having just tersely paraphrased the great passage of Plutarch in *The E at Delphi* 392: "La fleur d'âge se meurt et passe quand la vieillesse survient") that we are always changing, changing creatures in a world that changes about us as it changes in us, "both the judging and the judged in continual change and motion": "ainsi il ne se

---

[9] See Misch, 1:407, who suggests that even after the Paenetian refigurations of what individuality means "self-scrutiny took place not through the urge to make the individual depths visible, but in consequence of a changed, increasingly individual attitude to the ideas that existed independently of the particular life story." The individual still tells his story in order to accommodate himself to the ideal, that is, to approximate his living of his life as nearly as he can to the life of reason (to the universal prescription of a Plato or a Zeno, for instance); his "philosophy itself, with its mission of guidance in life, does not grow out of personal experience" but out of a "dogma" that tells him who he is and isn't. Self-representation (this is what Horace's fictions of self-portraiture gesture toward) tries to catch the surface as exactly as possible, because whatever depths there are will best be seen through that transparent skin. In a sense, this mimetic strategy reveals another perspective on the problem sketched in n. 5 on p. 90–92 above. See, for the problem with "self-knowing," Cic. *De or.* 3.33.

peut établir rien de certain." That, surely, ought to add up to "unpatterned randomness" and the anxiety that it occasions. But it doesn't. Montaigne went on till his last breath, with great enjoyment, trying (*experiens vir*) to pattern *le branlement* that both disturbed and delighted him. He didn't achieve a certain, clear, fixed, unchanging explanation of himself moving in the motions of the realities, because, as he insists, there is no such thing and there can be no such thing. For all that, he doesn't despair over this aporia (though he may lose his nerve or his patience from time to time because of it), nor does he rail against language and narrative because they've betrayed him (they haven't) or because they've failed to keep promises they made him (they made none). They never guaranteed him certainties about himself or anything; they only offered him good if limited tools (good if he worked hard with them), and, of course, he made enthusiastic and wonderful use of them. He told his story to everyone if anyone ever did, and he told it superbly—partly because he knew the big rules of narration: never stop telling the story, never be satisfied with the story you've told. Montaigne may have the honor of inventing or reinventing the essay (two of his favorites, Plutarch and Seneca, share the honor for ancient Greek and Latin), but, given his usual tone of voice and his constant revisions (he's like someone calling you back yet again late at night, "And one last thing I forgot to mention"), he seems also a sort of master epistler, one whose letters are no less to the world than Dickinson's. He never forgets his reader, not for an instant. No writer I know speaks to his readers so flawlessly, so steadily "as if to thee alone." As if waiting for an answer, for an affirmation, or, just as good or better, a denial. This unusually heightened sense of the listening, about-to-answer reader, this awareness of the other in Montaigne's essays, is of course a fiction, but it is a significant and an instructive fiction (rather than dust in the eyes or comfy fantasy). We cannot know ourselves by ourselves:

> O wad some Power the giftie gie us
> To see ourseles as others see us,

It wad frae monie a blunder free us
And foolish notion!

Burns's prayer is answered for us in our lives and for Horace in his *Epistles* by direct conversation with other people (our dialogic "readers") or by letters to and from them when direct conversation is not possible. (Alas, there it is again, the primacy of the living voice; admittedly, there are times when a letter is preferable to a conversation, but conversation remains the norm and the ideal.) When we talk to ourselves about ourselves, silently or aloud, on a walk or on paper, we may or may not succeed in having what amounts to having a good conversation with ourselves, depending on how honest we are trying to be with ourselves, how serene or integrated at the given moment we happen to be when self-conversing thus; in transforming monologue into something more like a dialogue, in writing a diary or journal, we may escape the dangers of solipsism in which our ordinary obsessions and anxieties construct their usual mannikins without being thwarted by friendly criticism. In conversing with others (lover, spouse, parent, friend, acquaintance, stranger, enemy), we may succeed in persuasively performing for them (foisting off on them) our favorite version of our selves (or we may merely think we have done this, mishearing their caveats or translating them into something that conforms to what we wanted them to say). But on balance it seems more likely that there will be a better chance for sound verification (or, if this is what decorum demands, refutation) of our story, this segment, this shred, of that long novel, our life, when we are talking with another than when we are attempting to make a dramatic monologue before the looking glass do duty for the give-and-take of show-and-tell followed by question and answer with that audience, the other. The religious hermit who abandons converse with his kind in the hopes of surviving the terror and pain of delving into his inner misery (his worthlessness) and of then moving beyond them into the contemplation of the gods beyond all misery can perhaps afford to risk the dementia of the bad silence that often attends on introspection. But most of us cannot.

The self that decides to look inside had better be prepared to turn its gaze outward at short notice and to be willing to look outside as much or more than it looks inside and finally to be content at last to discover the self's best likeness (approximation, *vraisemblance*) reflected in the faces, echoed in the voices, of its interlocutors. That version of the self, those versions of the self, those fragments of selves, will be short on unity, and in a way they will be no more susceptible of verification than the bright, clear, and illusory image that the self could have seen in the many-mirrored shrine of its own breast, but it will offer plausibilities that the lonely, secret, unsharable eidolon could never provide, and it will, of course, be blessed with companionship, with the answering voices and answering eyes that most of us, in some degree, most of the time, stand in need of. For although one high human ideal, and one of the fiercest and most persistent, may be that of *autarkeia,* most of us have no real talent for that supreme independence. We are, most of us, creatures of the campfire; we need friendly (or stern) words; we need helping hands and an occasional shoulder to weep on.

In choosing to write letters to the world that he had claimed to say more or less good-bye to, Horace admits that he is one of these, one of most of us. His dreams of autonomy and immaculate independence turn out to be little more than dreams; his freedom turns out to be contingent, imperfect, limited; his retirement (which was apparently to have been utter and final and complete) turns out to be partial. The self of the *Epistles* is the thing or, better, the process that sends the letters, that tells the part of the story each letter contains, that sends the snapshot that reveals things as they are at this moment in this place. The self tells a story of pain and boredom and fear that have driven it into retreat from the city and its accustomed haunts and habits, a story of conversion to a certain *askēsis* of healing and transformation, of progress perhaps toward the goal of that tendance of soul; a story of relapses and new caprices, of flights to new and false refuges, of moments of serenity and of balance, of forgotten resentments that suddenly reappear, of genial resignation and witty tolerance discovered and sustained, of humility glimpsed and desired. This story that the self tells is not only a construct by the self but *is* also the very self in its constant reconfigurations.[10]

Whether we decide the *Epistles,* this Horatian version of self-hood, is actually a picture of facets of a single self seen in the various mirrors that the recipients of the letters provide it with; or that these letters show us many selves in many mirrors appropriate to them; whether we say that the sum of these mirrored versions is the whole Horatian self (real or fictive or something betwixt and between); or that they merely gesture to an unknowable, uncompletable process, to a series of random fragments whose sum, were there such a thing, would still be less significant than any of its parts, to coruscations of incarnate spirit that artifice gathers into a radiant and ephemeral integrity—any or all of these qualifications, interesting though they might be, are nothing to my purpose here. They belong to the great, unending debate of all the centuries and continents and languages about the nature of the human soul. For my present purpose, it is enough to say that the self of these verse letters, telling its story (stories) to others in snatches, is in search of its serenity and its balance, and the unfinished (unfinishable) story of that search is what is being told here, in this way (letters), for this purpose: to escape from the Gorgon's mirror of solipsism and to attain, through advice, correction, and encouragement, the habits and the self-confidence that will allow for experimentation and for change, without which the new story cannot continue and without which the new teller cannot relearn his craft for the telling of the new tale(s).

He, the newest new teller, this strange creature, forty-three years old, no longer a satirist, no longer—he thinks—a lyricist,

---

[10] See Misch, 1:336, for Polybius's anxiety over and dismissal of inconsistency in human character, shrewd observer of inconsistency though he was; for too sober a discussion of Horace's knack for disunity of character, see McGann, 12–13. For instability and plurality of self as a topos in autobiography, see Olney, 11, 29.

now feeling, for the first time in a long while, a stranger in an alien world, a stranger in his skin, a stranger to himself. Horace, then, to say it once again, is not revealing who and what he is (as a movie star or politician might pretend, or attempt, to do in a television interview); he is trying to become what he is trying to imagine by thinking it through with other people (friends and nonfriends alike). This seeker and shaper and renewer is very different from the urbane, unshakable courtier that the eighteenth century devised and worshiped or from the Victorian Flaccus, a Herrick in a toga, licitly sensual and patriotic and pious, that the nineteenth century found it possible to tolerate and even to revere or from the smug, fatuous hypocrite on the make that his most recent traducer has discovered in him—these portraits of Flaccus are unified, have clear centers and clear outlines; they are finished personalities. The Horace I offer here is more like Montaigne or Goethe; he is "a man that is movement in movement."[11]

This penchant for dynamic transmutation (of self's care, of perspectives) tells us, I think, why he doesn't talk about progress—though he mentions it prominently—in the way we might expect him to.[12] Being motion in motion, he is not a stable thing moving from one stable point to another stable point, is not the

---

[11] See Reed, 53.

[12] E.1.32, 2.40, 7.96–97 (regression as progress); 10.42–43 (the shoe suggests locomotion, though admittedly this is stretching a point); 11.30 (the road not taken, as a sort of antiprogression); 13.1 (*proficiscentem* applied to Vinius suggests the spiritual journey of books into the royal presence, which smacks of metaliterary picaresque); 15.10 (the moral journeyer gone gaga); 17.4 (the blind leading the blind); 17.38 (*pervenit*, ironic journey's end); 19.2–22 (ironic use of *princeps*, appropriation of Stoic journey for "a life lived in literature" by a saint of Grub Street); 20.5–6 (the boybook's progress-regress). The first three instances are (or rather, seem to be) unironic fashionings of the topic, and as such they act as signals to the reader that what she is about to read, has begun to read, is a book about the testament of a pilgrim to the Goodness of the Way. Once the reader has got to 10 he may feel that the signals were mixed, mistaken, or downright fraudulent, which means that the early, "straightforward" allusions to the topos of the pilgrim become ambiguous as the book is unrolled. For the signals in question here, see Rabinowitz, 44, 76–93.

proficiens, going from the place and moment of his conversion to the place and moment of his satori. This is why he emphasizes his flaws, his relapses; why he admits to being *ventosus,* protean, less prone to outburst than before but still capable of resentment; why he can recall the moods and anxieties that set him on his journeys toward health (*caelum non animum*) and that had tempted him—the memory of that despair is bitter and fearful—to set up his prayer rug on the desolate promontory (*oblitus, obliviscendus,* "the world forgetting, by the world forgot," 11.9), where there would be no more letters to and from the wicked world outside, where there would be only the repetition, forever, of the single (and untrue) story of how he had been betrayed by the world and by himself.

These moments, it's true, are more than balanced by a sense of trust in the discordant concord, particularly toward the end of the collection—until, that is, the fury of the penultimate poem, 19, violently reechoes the earlier echoes of resentment, thereby reminding us of what it is he and we are escaping from. His capacity for gratitude for things as they are, and his gift for finding balance in himself for himself, his desire to retain and to refine his curiosity toward the world outside him and to enjoy the friends (and the foes, for in fact he never quite stopped being a satirist) who help make the world such a fascinating place—all this finally vanquishes the long, deep resentments of the rag and bone shop. The idea of learning to be a *proficiens* was initially attractive because it offered both a clear direction and a rough yet fairly certain mode of transportation (trudging barefoot up the sheer, rocky path to Virtue). But by the time the composition of the *Epistles* had begun to gather steam, that Stoic lucidity of direction and method began to seem rather specious. His problem was not to get from point A (he didn't know where that was) to point B (he especially didn't know where that was). His problem was to orient himself in that strange new landscape of the inner-outer self (a place, so it seemed, without satire or lyric) before he began his journey to selfhood (or away from it).

But then he begins to notice that each day is a new day, and each day's self is (in a sense, in Plutarch's sense, and Montaigne's) a possibly new self. He doesn't know either where he's going or, if he did, how to get there. So he takes to sitting by Vacuna's crumbling shrine or by the stream. Sitting in forgetfulness, *zho wang*. Doing by not doing, *wu wei*. Then he comes to have the sneaking hunch that perhaps he is among (or rather, "is") the 10,000 things in their constant permutations. So, he doesn't have to go anywhere, because he *is* going everywhere just by sitting where he sits. And he no longer has to worry about who he is, because he is everything: "If you hide the universe inside the universe, there's no room for it to get lost in." He takes to sunning himself a little longer; he grows a little greyer, a little pudgier, a little less irritable. This slow, imperceptible process doesn't overwhelm him, prostrate him, transform him: this is not the road to Damascus in any of its many metonymies. He continues to write letters, both those he wants to write to people he loves or likes and those he doesn't want to write to people he cares little for. He no longer has, moreover, an absolute need to stay in the country. He can go back to Rome from time to time when need or inclination suggests that he go there. By ceasing to worry how his skin fits him he has become at home in it, maybe for the first time in his life, or for the first time since his wonderful and crazy father snatched him up from a place he felt he belonged in and carted him off to a place he loathed and feared (and learned to love, and then learned to loathe and fear again). By giving himself up, by throwing up his hands in despair (as it had seemed) over making sense of himself and the world, he began to become himself. And now stays or goes as necessity or whim bids him go or stay. How does one go about structuring that, how can one pattern that dim, wavering, unfinished and unfinishable, business into intelligibility and lucid sequence?

One can't, and he doesn't try to. Sitting by Vacuna's shrine, sunning himself after a swim in the cool stream, dictating letters, regarding the quiet world about him, pondering memory and desire, becoming himself: that process is invisible, immeasurable, unrepresentable. What he gives us to evoke this force-field of the psyche is snapshots of various moments in the process, presented in no privileged order, and this achronological but not synchronic spectrum of moments, none of them (except perhaps the first) redolent of *peripeteia,* may evoke in his readers' minds and hearts some likenesses of what such a strange, almost atemporal, almost aspatial transformation might be.[13] Though I would suggest that poems 17 and 18 hint that there has been some movement forward from the opening sketch of the spiritual crisis that generates the verse letters (or if there was no such crisis in the poet's life, the one he imagines and lets his other poems grow from), I can't detect any interest or intention on the poet's part in graphing that process or progress from the first poem in the collection to and through poems 17 and 18. I think that the poems can in fact be read effectively in a linear way (this reading will in effect transform the collection into a spatial pattern, a static frieze or series of panels, perhaps like the Lucilian life, as Horace describes his experience in reading it, S.2.1.32f., and this linear version might even be made to yield a chronological, progressive pattern for all I know); but the *Epistles* can also be read in what seems to me a dynamic pattern, in a way that paradoxically ignores linear motion and diminishes the significance of sequence in order to emphasize what might be called thematic motion, thematic dynamism, the zigzag of the correspondences and oppositions of key words and key themes throughout the collection, the play and counterplay of the poet's tone as he addresses friend or not-friend, the movement in time, not *to* a goal at the end of the collection but *in* a consummation of all the themes and variations, all the concords and discords, a hidden resolution that is seen to be everywhere in the poems once our personal performance of them (our reading of them) is completed—just at the moment when the unfinished life, the uncompleted pilgrimage, explodes like fireworks in 20 and disappears. All meaningful motion is not in a straight line. There is the motion of a Hamiltonian cycle on a star-

---

[13] Abrams, 225–37, provides a radical example of the genre in his discussion of the spiritual autobiography of Hegel *proficiens-perfectus.*

shaped graph, for instance, and there are also the travels of the Eskimo:

> In describing a distant place . . . an Eskimo will often make no reference to the mass of land between (which would impress us and which we would describe in terms of distance), but only to geographical points, and not necessarily seen from the point of one's approach. Thus, to a non-Eskimo observer, the Eskimo might seem to have no sense of direction. And because he travels somewhat like an arctic fox, turning aside to investigate something unusual or moving in a series of steps punctuated by short stops for tea, instead of a straight, relentless dash for a goal, the Eskimo might be thought poorly self-disciplined or improvident. But it would only have to do with how the Eskimo saw himself in the fabric of space and time and how he conceived of "proceeding" through the world, where he placed lines or points in the stream of duration.[14]

If the Stoically or Platonically prescribed itinerary seems not to suit one's experience or temperament or both, perhaps one should journey like the Eskimo. If one has ceased to be obsessed with telling stories about the past (where one came from) or inventing stories about the future (where one is going and why); if, instead, one has begun to notice more and more what surrounds one here and now, has begun to live as much as possible in the present (without irresponsibly abandoning what matters in the past or may matter in the future); if, the more one is gathered into the nowness and hereness of things and people outside oneself, one ceases to need to look so much within, ceases to worry quite so much about who one is, one may very well sit more frequently by Vacuna's shrine or half doze in the sunlight on the bank of the cool stream, remembering what one likes about one's friends, thinking less and less about what one dislikes about Rome or the inmates of its corridors of power. No more mad flights from Rome to the farm, from the farm to Rome,

[14] Lopez, 57.

from the farm down the coast in pursuit of health or serenity in some new place. Now the slow walk through familiar scenery and some visits to the city. This might seem, to the ignorant observer, like a listless, futile sort of way to travel: going no-where and going there not very fast. But it gets you where you're going if where you are is eternity.

In one of the briefest letters, 8, to Celsus, Horace tells his Muse to answer a possible question from the recipient of the letter about his health by saying he is not well-off: *dic multa et pulchra minantem / vivere nec recte nec suaviter,* "Tell him that though I make lots of lovely promises, I am living my life neither pleas-antly nor well," 3–4. Not because his health is poor or the farm is having a run of bad luck, *sed quia mente minus validus quam corpore toto / nil audire velim, nil discere, quod levet aegrum,* "but because, sicker in spirit than I am anywhere in my entire body, I prefer to hear nothing, to learn nothing that might alleviate my sickness," 7–8. He blows up at doctors who are trying to cure him; he furiously demands to know of his friends why they're so bent on trying to coax him out of his deadly stupor. *quae nocuere sequar, fugiam quae profore credam, / Romae Tibur amem, ventosus Tibure Romam,* "I scurry after anything that will do me harm and run like hell from anything that might help me. When I'm in Rome I long to be in Tibur, when I'm in Tibur I crave to be in Rome," 11–12.

Ventosus? Windy, capricious, random, moods in their unpre-dictable swinging. The invalid guesses that he is (rudely) talking too much to himself. He therefore asks Celsus how he's doing in the service of Tiberius. If he answers *recte,* the Muse is to congrat-ulate him and then immediately whisper this qualification into his ear: *ut tu fortunam, sic nos te Celse feremus,* "We'll deal with you, Celsus, as you deal with your luck," 17. *recte* = I'm doing OK. Celsus's anticipated response echoes the *recte* of 4, where Horace says that he is very definitely *not* doing OK. I'm OK, you're OK? Perhaps Celsus isn't doing quite as well as he imagines. Maybe no self can be happy (as the world ordinarily imagines happi-ness). This is the bitterest and most concentrated statement of dissatisfaction with self in the letters, and its bitterness heightens Horace's rejection of the hive, of the world of power and mindless prosperity that Celsus and his desire for that world symbolize. But the poem's chief function, for our immediate purposes, is to give a powerful expression to the theme of painful, bad, neurotic volatility, a theme that the second part of the book will develop, a *mal* (an evil and a pain) toward whose ultimate cure (outside the book, outside its story) the spirit of the book gestures.

In 11, just after the luminous moment when Horace is finishing the dictation of his letter to Fuscus at Vacuna's shrine, the theme of the anxiety of journeying is taken up again. Like Horace, Bullatius has itchy feet. He has been abroad; in asking him about his tour in the East, Horace takes the opportunity of recalling his own visit to Lebedus (*Gabiis desertior atque / Fidenis vicus,* "a hamlet more desolate than Gabii or Fidenae," 7–8), and the memory of that desolation stirs in him thoughts of his persistent inclination to try to escape, to escape into the wilderness, into "the desolation of reality": *tamen illic vivere vellem / oblitusque meorum, obliviscendus et illis, / Neptunum procul e terra spectare furentem,* "But that's where I wanted to stay—the memory of it is so strong in me that I seem, at this moment, to be back there and then, wanting to forget my friends and be forgotten by them, looking out from the shore on the fury of Neptune," 8–10. In other words, locked into the desolation he feels inside himself, he remembers the place Bullatius visited recently, a place so barren and empty of humankind that, imagining himself returned there, he wants (again) never to leave it, so exact is the image it presents to him of what he finds within himself. Yes, there are times when *odio maris atque viarum* ("from our disgust with the sea and with roads," 6), weary of travel and of life itself, we want to take refuge in such a place. When we've spent our time searching for health or happiness in a change of scene, tried to discover health in many scenic changes, we may very well try to prove the actuality of our exhaustion and despair and self-hatred, finding outward signs for inner spiritual states, by choosing to settle down in the grimmest place we can come on. But what we must learn (that is, teach ourselves) is that the frenzied junkets result from a profound confusion of what's really hurting us and where our happiness really is, what it really is. Once we see that our desire is insatiable when it is for things outside us, once we see that we have what we need inside us, we have reached our journey's end. And then the real journey can begin. *caelum non animum mutant qui trans mare current. / strenua nos exercet inertia* ("We change our whereabouts not our hearts when we speed across the sea; our energetic idleness wears us out," 27–28). We rush about looking for how to live well, but what we want is right here, *quod petis hic est, est Ulubris, animus si te non deficit aequus* ("and you can even find it in any hick town anywhere—if you have a balanced spirit, a heart-mind that lives in the eternal now," 29–30). *tu quamcumque deus tibi fortunaverit horam / grata sume manu neu dulcia differ in annum* ("Make sure you take with a grateful hand whatever hour the god has gifted you with, and don't postpone your pleasures 'to another year,'" 22–23).

That is the secret, staring him in the face, that is what allows him to end this poem, as he ends 18, with what is now in effect his *sphragis*, his seal: *grata manu*. The balanced heart that seals the poem is rooted in gratitude, acceptance; in acceptance of things as they are, in gratitude for the lavish munificence of reality, of existence, of nature (for my money, the tone here is joyously Epicurean): take it and live it, richly, humbly, fully! Grateful for the day, with grateful hand! The ministers of grateful hedonism are *ratio* and *prudentia* (25), a claim that may irritate puritans of various kinds: good, clear thinking and a sense of what is likely to result from one's balancing of choices. It is intelligence and instinct that ward off *curas*, anxieties, depressions, sick delusions.

This statement of genuine *aequitas* is as perfect as was the evocation of its absence in 8. In a less honest version of the *Epistles*, this poem and the great prayer that ends 18 might come together at the end of the volume. So, in *Anna Karenina*, Tolstoy's own repressed fears and uncertainties prompt him to bestow on Levin a secular salvation and thus to bring a "happy" closure to a novel that nevertheless continues to resonate with the tragic precision of Anna's fight for freedom and truth. I don't, of course, mean that Tolstoy's novel is a lesser book than the *Epistles;* this greatest of novels is so powerful that it triumphs over its sentimental and inadequate "rounding off." Levin's struggle, which counterpoints Anna's, will be honestly resolved only in *Resurrection* and *What Then Must We Do?* and in those last incredible stories about suffering and injustice. Tolstoy had tried to avoid writing those later, terrifying works by making Levin happy. Horace doesn't make this mistake.

In 15, to Vala, just before the trio of poems that leads up to the prayer, we find him dealing once again with the inconstancy of human personality and the inadequacy of resolutions and of doctrine alike. He is back to rushing around the peninsula looking for health, sleep, and happiness in all the wrong places, doing anything and everything rather than confront the malformed desire that drives him to look for sanity where it can't be found. A flirtation with gluttony that seems to accompany this game of changing places (*mutandus locus est et diversoria nota / praeteragendus equus,* "I've got to change my surroundings and spur my horse past the familiar spas," 10–11) puts him in mind of another dedicated eater, Maenius, of whom he gives us a brief description: *scurra vagus, . . . pernicies et temptestas barathrumque macelli,* "a parasite-at-large, . . . the bane of the supermarket, its whirlwind, its abyss," 28–31. Sometimes, when this monster is forced to dine cheaply (but plentifully), having somehow and suddenly become a moral paragon (*correctus Bestius,* 37), he rebukes those who, like himself, have literally eaten up their inheritances, but then, just as suddenly, unable to maintain this posture (this resolve, as it were), he slides back into his vice of choice and starts devouring delicacies. His sketch of Maenius completed, Horace dryly remarks, *nimirum hic ego sum!,* "That's me to a T," 42. But the similarity has less to do with gourmandizing than with relapsing: *nam tua et parvula laudo, / cum res deficiunt, satis inter vilia fortis,* "When I'm short of cash, I extol the virtues of a secure frugality, a man of steel morals when I'm down at the heels," 42–

43. But he changes his tune quickly when there's a turn for the better. We are all of us, Horace no less than Maenius, creatures of contingency—and when we forget that, when we confuse who we are with what surrounds us, then we become essentially the reflection of what happens at the moment to be our circumstances, whatever identity we may have or think we have at the moment when our luck changes.

Here, just as the book is about to move into its complex recapitulations of its major themes (freedom, dependence, identity, balance), the psyche's imperfections and its fluid dialectical motions are definitively stressed. Which is the true statement, or the more nearly true statement—this admission of failure and fragmentation and inadequacy, *hic ego sum,* "Yep, that's me," the creature of conflicting desires and feeble resolutions, the changeable configuration of will and appetite that is finally incapable of a complete and final change for the better? Is that the real Horace of these poems, of this book of letters? Or is it the Horace who prays for the chance to find for himself an *aequus animus* at the end of 18 and who avows the possibility of the ethical reality of that soul at the end of 11 and who, in later years, will lay claim, almost, to having almost grasped that equity in *E.2.2*?

Both Horaces are the real Horace (of the poems at least); both versions are true versions, since both represent an aspect of the paradoxical and mysterious reality that is the human personality. There is, whether really or potentially, a core to the personality which remains (in a sense) constant through all its changes: the I that says, I do not live *recte;* I must seek, I am seeking, my good; I am trying to become what I truly am (*in potentia*). And there is also a part of the personality that experiences transformation; that observes keenly the differences between what it was and what it is, between what it had been being and what it is on the verge of becoming; then learns to mark off the differences between these "moments" and what it still yearns to become. The first aspect is, in a sense, permanent; the second is, in a sense, never the same. Each of these aspects is somehow, in their unities and in their discontinuities with each other, oneself. An oxy-

moron that catches at some of this strangeness (this almost un-
thinkableness) is Goethe's word for the permanence in change
and the change in permanence that marks the rainbow created by
the waterfall that Faust looks upon at the opening of part 2 of his
vast journey: *Wechseldauer*. This word and the monologue's closing verse, which completes the sense of its image, "Am farbigen
Abglanz haben wir das Leben," "Our lives partake of an iridescent reflection," give us some hold on the duality-become-unity
of *hic ego sum*. Something that abides, something that glints
too briefly, too vividly, too complexly to be truly seen and
thereby truly understood. Something that reason and language
have some share in and something that (*simul*) far outstrips their
enormous powers and their shared and separate realms. So, paradox, oxymoron, *concordia discors*. The self that changes and does
not change. The self that progresses and simultaneously (almost)
regresses, loops back on itself. The self that needs the city, the self
that can thrive only in the country. The self that is free and the self
that can, equally, never be free.[15]

Looking out at Soracte and its snow, looking out at the raging
sea, he has seen something that neither Socrates nor Aristippus
nor Diogenes could see, or, to say it more plainly, something
they would not bother to see, since to see it would be to sanction
it and in the process to demote the city and the truth of conversation, of debate, of "conjectures and refutations." To have stayed
out there permanently, to remain there, gazing ever more deeply
into the glare and the tumult (should we say, into the sublime?)
might have created calm in the heart, would have diminished the
sense of self in torment, and that would have been for the better
temporarily but not for the best finally. So Horace doesn't do
that. He returns to the city where his real teachers—Socrates, the
Cyrenaics, the Cynics—learned among the crowds, in rough
questioning and rougher answer, in pleasure and freedom, that
we can never know ourselves well enough—and must never stop
trying to. But he doesn't stay put in the city either; he returns,

---

[15] See Stack, 288.

maybe more and more frequently, to silence and to the pictures of serenity that his farm and what circles it proffer him. But now when he walks in his gardens or into the wildness beyond them, he no longer imagines that he has won, here, pure freedom. He remembers both who he is and how this farm—on which such freedom as he enjoys depends—came to be his.

When various distresses had driven him (luckily) to say, I will, I would, I could give it all back, he learned that he wouldn't do that.[16] He learned that he wasn't Diogenes any more than he was the spineless sycophant that envious critics and his own guilt accused him of being. It was then, one day or another, when walking in that free and unfree garden, that he felt it suddenly flash on him that he could write about how one struggles to become free and how that daily fight to escape whatever enslaves us and to become who we were born to be is never finished and always beyond us but is nevertheless the thing we want most in life, and is, despite its continual evasions of us, something that, if we truly understand it (among other things, like happiness, it is not a thing to be possessed, but an action), never disappoints us and that, if we don't try to control it and hoard it up, if we learn to take it as it's given, *grata manu,* never fails us.

[16] He did, of course, give *everything* back, everything material that his having become a regular in the salon of Maecenas had brought to him over the years. Maecenas was dead by the time it was time for this gesture of bequeathing, so Horace's heir, perhaps because his feelings were hurt if the dying thought badly of him or did not think of him at all (Suet. *Aug.* 77), was, inevitably and ironically, Augustus. For the meaning of the salon, see P. White's brilliant reconstruction of what the Augustan salon was, in particular: 1978, 78, 84–86, 92; 1982, 56, 65; and his forthcoming *Promised Verse: Poet and Poetry in the Society of Augustan Rome.*

[6]

GARDENS

But beyond the hills? Eh?
Perhaps it's still green. Eh?
Flora! Pomona! Ceres!

—Samuel Beckett

Musonius Rufus, that sanest of the Neronian Stoics, in his fragment 11, "On Suitable Means of Earning a Living for a Philosopher," explicitly relegates sophists to the city, which allows him to find—Socrates, for one, would be surprised—a very natural habitat for philosophers in the countryside, on the farm. The farmer's vocation embraces an honest way of making a living, decides Musonius, an opinion we have already encountered (above, p. 50) in Cato's introduction to his book of agriculture, and since there are few honest ways to earn a living (as Stoics view the matter), this is a decisive advantage for the philosophical life, even if there were no others: but there *are* other advantages hardly less important than this one. Farming provides the kind of leisure that the philosopher needs (perhaps he means the sort of enforced, relative leisure some farmers enjoy in off-season, but even so, most real, as against gentlemanly, philosophical, farmers— Cato very audible among them—would have a thing or two to tell him about farming and *scholē*, as doubtless would his slaves). Furthermore, according to Musonius, the farmer's life gives the philosopher a chance to be with his pupils at almost every moment of the day (his students, it would seem, make up a sort of serendipitous work force, trading muscle and sweat for instruction), and this happy reciprocity permits him to teach them by constant example, as well as by discourse, what virtue in action is. (Is there here some taut antinomy of leisure versus exemplary labor that needs a deconstructionary hand to [dis]solve it, or could we say that perhaps the philosopher talks virtuously while his students toil, or can we admit that, in this perspective, the absence of the city and its noise and temptations and corruptions is equivalent to *scholē* and that thinking—even thinking out loud, lecturing, inciting disputation and sustaining it—is not incompatible with physical labor?)

Peculiar as this fragment is if judged by Greek standards—except for Hesiod and perhaps for Xenophon the Greek farmer is an uncultivated, dim-witted hayseed—it suits the agrarian core of the Roman *Weltbild* and *Wortwelt* perfectly. There are several moments in *De senectute,* for instance, as well as in the *Georgics,* when it seems clear that one would, in this world, have a much better chance of encountering a philosopher-farmer than a philosopher-king, and one has only to look at a few pages of Tolstoy's *What Then Must We Do?* and to think of that book's extraordinary renewals in Gandhi and in Martin Luther King, Jr., and in liberation theology to see that the idea is possessed both of an elemental vitality and a genuine nobility.

Though personally not persuaded by Musonius's argument, I am confident of its purity of will ("purity of will is to wish one thing"), and I recall it because that purity points up what I take to be the paradox (in a way, the good impurity, the exact ambivalence) of Horace's picture of his fictive/real self in the *Epistles:* having found himself on the farm (having found, on the farm, the difficulties of finding himself), having decided, however, not to stay there permanently and irrevocably, he decides to make the farm, a real/fictive scene of the dialectical struggle that the composition of the *Epistles* is rooted in, his base point, the center of the balanced, variously and capriciously yet genuinely dis-

ciplined, living of his life (another cop-out, the rustic purist
mutters; another typically Peripatetic or Stoic-Cynic or Cynic-
Cyrenaic or heretically Epicurean dilution, mumbles the cosmopolitan sybarite).

His letter to his bailiff confirms our intuition that there are no
Stoic disciples down on the farm, waiting in the furrows or in the
dairy to be Catonized (nor is it a question of young converts who
need the finishing touches for their Epicureanization or even
their hedonization), and most of what goes on in the *Epistles*
tends to suggest that Musonius wouldn't approve of the life that's
being lived there. It's a poet's life, not a philosopher's, that's
blossoming "out in the country" (new blossoms on an old bush),
but more than that, and far more irritating to Musonius and
apparently to some of his latter-day, perhaps unwitting, followers, it is also in many ways, at least by the time the letters are
being written, the life of a modern sophist.

What is a sophist doing on a farm instead of, decorously,
pounding the pavements; buttonholing unwary interlocutors;
threatening to deface the coinage with a view to restoring some
value to it once its encrustations have been attended to (Diogenes
is, for all his peculiar genius, in the tradition of the sophists);
"making people uncomfortable in their skins" (so a later sophist,
as a very young man, Nietzsche, would prophetically describe
his life's work as he then envisioned it); revealing to the as-
tonished victims (and beneficiaries) of sophistry, willing and
unwilling alike, how the words they speak really sound, how
little they actually correspond to what they were intended to
convey? Perhaps it is the sheer perversity of his somewhat acci-
dental situation (falling between two stools; being, amphibi-
ously, of the city and country; becoming, being revealed as, an
agrarian sophist) that pleased Horace about "ending up," more or
less, on the farm, almost as though he had guessed that eventually some Stoic or other would demand that only genuine,
fully committed philosophers (not poets dabbling parodically
with the erotics of wisdom—not to mention the anxieties of
"green thoughts in a green shade") should be permitted to style

themselves (gentlemen) farmers; perhaps, after the oddities of his circumstances became clear to him, he deliberately positioned himself, like a naughty scarecrow, as cautionary émblem of the inevitable Musonian prescription-proscription.[1] But such delight in discrepancy, in flouting those ersatz decorums, would be only part of the reason the sophist became—if not quite a farmer—a part-time gardener.

Civilization and its discontents! The antinomies (both real and only apparent) of nature and culture, *physis* and *nomos!* How did Flaccus, amateur gardener (and, in a way, amateur sophist as well), how did he grapple with them? How did he learn to live with them? The *Epistles* is the achronic, unnarrativized record (real or fictive or not quite either and not quite both, something betwixt and between) of how he did that. And how he did it shows resemblances (unextraordinary ones once the kinships are acknowledged) to the "methods" of such reconciliations in others of his kind, from Socrates and Protagoras to Erasmus and Montaigne, from Erasmus and Montaigne to—(but readers should, by the rules of the game, supply their own examples of modern or current or postmodern sophistic individualists with what one might call, in the teeth of technocratic prejudices and neocon misgivings, humanistic leanings). He did it by acknowledging the existence and the power of the antinomy, by accepting it, *by not denying* its reality, its central place and meaning, in human life and human experience. Civilization's kings (general/priest/judge) and their shamans do deny this antinomy. For them, inevitably and, for the most part, unhypocritically, this antinomy makes their work essentially impossible. They must have warrant for what they say; they must have authorization for—giving commands. No such warrant, no such authorization, is possible

---

[1] For an interesting effort to describe the Stoic attempt to usurp the garden of Epicurus, see Morford: it is to green quietudes that Stoics, exhausted by the task of reforming reality, retire from time to time to heal their shattered nerves—the garden of Epicurus, of course, is located in the city, beyond whose walls the sounds of urban discord, though muffled, can be clearly heard.

unless there is a clear, or at least an adequate, correspondence between *res* and *verba*. For commands to have meaning there must be something behind them, and, moreover, their meaning (their purpose) must be (or at least must seem) as unequivocal as their origin. Without some degree of sufficient exactitude in the relating of things and the words that token them, the work that makes civilization work cannot be carried on. The kings and their shamans may, for various reasons, come to feel that these correspondences are not quite genuine, that the stories that validate them are dubious, that what seemed (and must continue to seem) natural turns out to be more nearly conventional (that is to say, constructed, not born, from nature), that all the facts in which life is rooted turn out to be, are revealed as being—not when we look at them and prod them, but when we talk about them or our prodding and our looking—fictions. When this occurs, and it seems to do so with considerable regularity, what is called for is some variety of untruth, one that is at once noble and beautiful. It is at this point in this recurring story that the sophist is likely to make his appearance.

Sophists come in all shapes and sizes (not to mention classes, genres, and genders). What seems to characterize them as a group (aside from their conventional role in the conventional story of culture that I sketch) is their sensitivity to and obsession with how people talk, that is to say, with how people use, and are used by, language. Here are some crucial aspects of this obsession. (1) There is a passion, a craving, for correct or adequate or amusing or revolutionary predication, some overwhelming, ineluctable conviction that for life to be lived (as against got through) the grammarians and lexicographers—not to mention the scientists and technocrats—must have their trees shaken or the cages in their prison houses rattled (this is perhaps the Socratic specialty). (2) There must be (here we find Prodicus's hobbyhorse) an obsession with *akribologia*,[2] a disdain for the illusion of synonyms, a crazed appetite for distinguishing among shades that at first

2 See Kerford, 69–71.

appear to have, between and among them, no genuine distinctions, a crying need to "uncrumple much-crumpled things." (3) There is often, but not regularly, a Gorgianic interest in making sure that the structures—ornaments they are not—of discourse be as entertaining as possible, that they be richly furnished with answering and with discordant "echoes and mirrors," that they be as capable as can be of challenging the mind to work in and with a given discourse through its complexities, instead of trying to skim through them in order to come upon and then ingest some imagined, predetermined kernel (or, as Woolf wittily keeps calling it, "nugget") they are thought to conceal (as if discourse were information and data rather than question and argument, *sic et non;* as if discourse were not as much about scrutinizing the nature and the meaning of information as it is about examining or displaying whatever information it might be engaged with; as if discourse itself were only or essentially truth or truths or wisdom or opinions, misinformation, disinformation, inadvertent error, facts bare and facts opaque). This Gorgianic obsession with style or figures has, of course, no special affiliation with "the baroque" or indeed with any level or kind of "style" and is as likely to manifest itself as Doric severity or Hemingway telegram as Asiatic feathers, fronds, and fireworks. Finally, (4), there is always, coexisting with Protagoras's tough yet evenhanded skepticism, a profound belief—no, it is a genuine faith—in the powers of language to help make human life livable, a faith that remains hale and vital only if it is always tested and thereby always renewed, only if, that is, it remains as flexible as the world it attempts to perceive and, ideally, as varied and as changing as the experiences that are registered behind the eye that attempts to perceive those experiences through the filter of language.

It goes without saying that language seems to change irrespective of the interventions of kings and their shamans on the one hand and of sophists (and other malcontents) on the other; yet at least some of its most crucial changes seem to result from the dialectical interplay of these two groups, in their efforts, on the one hand, to arrest the shiftings of language and, on the other, to facilitate those shiftings. At the level of hegemonic codes (but inevitably at the levels of private speech as well) this give-and-take between civilization and those who represent its discontents (the perennial sophist) seems very influential in shaping the ways that language, together with the choices and actions and patterns that language calls into being, will grow, and therefore in determining how vital that growth will be, how fertile, how blessed.

Seen from this vantage, language is more nearly like a garden than it is like, say, a *Zwang,* or a prison house. Language is indeed like a prison house, in some ways, at some times, in some places, but, then, it is also like a temple treasury or like a fortress or like a museum or like—like all sorts of things, depending on who is using it, for what purposes: its aspects and its functions are varied; it cannot be gathered into some fixed essence—unless one were to say, evoking essence to deny it, language is among the clearest of pluralism's mirrors. For my present purpose, which is to try to sum up my readings of the *Epistles,* it is the similarity between language and gardens that I want to examine (knowing full well that organic metaphors have, in this era of the higher technic, been disassembled or carted off to the warehouse).

Venio nunc ad voluptatem agricolarum, "I come now to the pleasure of farmers" (*De senectute* 25). Gardens have several functions, none of which can be entirely or permanently privileged over the others. They are useful (and necessary—or were so until quite recently, and may be so again); they are beautiful; they encourage work that is good for the soul (as well as producing nourishment both soul and body need); they furnish a suitable place for physical repose and also an atmosphere conducive to solace, to relaxation of the mind and the heart, to reflection, to meditation.[3] In the Roman version of the garden, there is no more question of nature's being mastered than of its being outwitted or circum-

---

[3] See O'Loughlin, in particular 9–10, for a discussion of this topic; this version of humanistic leisure is enormously and unequivocally respectful toward the claims of genteel retirement; it is haunted by the phantom of one of Aristotle's least happy inventions, *eleutheros ho hautou heneka, Metaph.* 982b.

vented. Nature is being struggled with or cooperated with, as the occasion requires, is being cajoled and placated, as we see in the great prayers of the Roman farmers of which Cato gives us a soupçon.[4] But it was also being—what?—not tamed, not used, not manipulated, not transformed (and not destroyed). None of these words, together with metaphors that sustain them, suggests what it is that a good gardener does with or to or for nature. *Persuades* takes us perhaps in the right direction. A gardener persuades by rearranging, by transplanting, by grafting, clipping, weeding, watering. He reorders what is given, that is, what he is able to do, in terms of his own complex and various needs and desires and purposes; he depends on what nature gives in the way of soil and seeds and weather. By following (to employ, briefly, the Stoic metaphor) nature's lead (by responding faithfully to its "laws" and chances and changes), while at the same time looking to achieve his own aims, the gardener creates and sustains a kind of harmony or balance, a kind of spiritual equity between himself and the natural world which is at once (mysteriously) outside of him and also (not less mysteriously) inside of him. Respecting both the potentialities and limitations of what he is working with (nature and himself), asking neither too much nor too little either of nature or of himself, slowly learning and never forgetting that neither failure nor success is very likely to be permanent, any good gardener will discover something about the dialectical relationship between luck and work, between contingency and freedom, between rule and whim, between nature and culture, that even the most gifted logician or the most adept historian might never quite come upon.

The garden is not a utopia, not a bed of roses. It is not, except on occasion, a place of repose where Aristotle's great contemplator looks out on the clear eternities clearly. It is a rough (if fascinating) place where you earn your keep (not to mention your sanity) by doing your work when it's time to work and enjoying the fruits of your labors when it's time for that. You are

---

[4] For what *natura* meant to Romans, see Ross, 19–20, 93, 102, 236–37.

free in the garden to do a variety of things as you want to do them as long as you don't—deluded by rumors of absolute freedom off in the trackless forest or off in the free-for-all cosmopolis— learn to disdain the garden or, worse, learn to despair of it. You are free in the garden as long as you keep in mind the terms and the limitations and the aims of your freedom.

The garden is, as Horace discovered in his art and perhaps in his life, a mean between extremes (wasteland/cosmopolis), but to say that is misleading if one succeeds only in summoning up the demon of mediocrity (for example, the suburb, which has the defects of both the virtues, the too little humanity/the too much humanity, that it offers to mediate between). In the dialectic of the mean there aren't three terms (two vices and their mediating virtue), but four terms. In the formulation that concerns us there are two opposites, two opposing evils, chaos and the hive, the wilderness and the technocracy, representing an excessive fluidity (or spontaneity) on the one hand and an excessive structuring (or discipline) on the other. Between these two evils or vices (these defects/excesses: defect of order, excess of liberty; defect of liberty, excess of order) are two goods, each of them bearing some resemblance to the evil it stands nearest to nature. On the one hand there is nature, which is akin to disorder in its partiality to fertility and extravagance and flux and variation; on the other, there is culture, which is akin to technocracy in its partiality to pattern, to change for the sake of change (technical virtuosity inventing the need for change, calling this improvement, *Schlimmbesserung* masquerading as Progress), to forms of unbridled and sometimes violent rationality (Dr. Teller's, for example) that are at once self-righteous and intolerant of whatever smacks of the—not humanistic or mystical or emotional, and *not* antirational either or irrational. There seems to be no word left for it—heart's reason, the reasons of the heart—so utterly has the Engineer as Savior[5] come to dominate our dictionaries, our cur-

---

[5] See Johnson, 1992. I am using "garden" as a sort of universal and unchanging symbol of various humanisms (Erasmus's among others) that I hope will survive, in some fashion, when humankind has completed its

riculum, our language. Nor is there a word, in English or in Latin, that I know of, for the fusion or harmony of nature and culture, a fusion or harmony that does not offer to synthesize or to mediate between chaos and technocracy but that escapes the evils they promote by maintaining a creative, dialectical balancing in which the virtues of both the defects, the spontaneity and the patterning, cohere. One thing the *Epistles* does is to supply the want of this single term ("rational freedom," for various sad reasons, won't do either) by giving us, in the hidden and achronological tale of Horace's struggle for freedom, in his evocation of the relationship that the city and the country come to form inside his soul as a result of that struggle, an image, the Horatian farm refined beyond its sketches in the first lyric collection, that has haunted and blessed the literature and culture of the West for two millenia.

Horace's garden resembles in many ways the rural, agrarian Italies we find in Cicero's great portrait of Cato the Elder, in Vergil's *Georgics,* in Pliny the Elder's tender, passionate, brilliant evocations of his personal deity, Terra-Natura-Italia (e.g., 3.39–42, 37.201). When his father took him away from Venusia, apparently just a few years before Caesar crossed the Rubicon, the

---

reconstructions of itself, having finally listened to what Lewis Mumford, among others, was trying to tell it about its dwindling interest in the valid projects of the enlightenment and about its love affair with bad technologies. But "garden," of course, is not universal and changeless in its various representations and constructions, and there are more fashions and functions in gardens through space-times than there are adjectives to qualify the bare noun. Horace's "gardens," in any case, have nothing to do with those that the system of signs examined by Zanker, 284–90, gesture toward and prescribe. For a good description of some ways *garden* has been de/re/constructed, particularly in the Thatcherian mode to jibe with *its* eternal verities, see Immirzi; the same topic finds cool scrutiny by Chambers, 32–37 (who, 14, quotes the immortal words "The lesson of the Falklands is that Britain has not changed"; Grenada, anyone?). What is perhaps sentimental or inadequately sincere (I'm an ardent urbanite without even a window box) about my effort to (mis)appropriate the image can be clearly glimpsed in Baudrillard's meditation ("Nature is never more exalted than when it is universally destroyed") on nature "recycled," 1990, 65–66.

country boy gradually became citified, and, perhaps even before he headed off to Athens and Philippi and to the military and political disenchantments they had waiting for him, he had discovered there, in the new Rome, that new and very un-Roman urbanity that in fact suited his first and, in a sense, native language (my hunch is that it was Greek and that his roots were in the Near East—shall we, this time round, make him Syrian?). But then, a decade later maybe, more slowly than his transformation from hick to city slicker or from alien to citizen, a strange reversal began, and he, the urbanite from points east, began to succumb not so much to the antique gravities of the Roman farm as to the enduring delights of the Italian countryside. Cicero and Vergil were right: the rural beauties and the rural calm of Italy were *that* magical and soothing and healing. He asked Maecenas for a farm (for a rather luxurious one, in fact, that may have been beyond his means), or Maecenas offered him one; and there he found not only the true glories of Italy (not of Rome, not of the hive) but also Epicurus's garden in a version where the *askēsis* of Epicurus, so sufficiently unchanged as to be eventually recognizable, was divested of its surlier dogmatisms, was softly tempered by Aristippean realities, was revised and reissued in the calm and flux, in the violence and clarity, of a nature experienced directly, constantly, with a delicate and carefully controlled suspension of intellectual demands and preconceptions. It became a place in which one could brood on self and on the languages of self. It became a place where—when the lyrics were finished and when he seemed about to be losing himself, to be entering a new kind of depression, to be descending into a sour and immutable sense of endings (his art, his life)—it became a place where he began to write the *Epistles*.

Into the countryside, maybe along with volumes containing various introductions to philosophy (and maybe also with malicious and affectionate thoughts of poor, wonderful Vergil, off somewhere in his own hideaway, agonizing not over the introductions to but over the dreadful intricacies of the dreadful primary texts themselves) he had brought, in his head, in his heart, an untranscendental version of Socrates, together with Diogenes and Bion and, as wicked and irreverent as any of them, the chameleon, Aristippus. That is to say, he brought with him into rural retirement not a set of theatrical poses suitable to one who dons the garland of repose but the critical spirit and a sense of how language changes and how the soul that uses language also changes, of how those two kinds of change supplement and support each other. And he came to see how the old Greekling streetsmart badgerings of words and meanings could connect (in his head) with the traditions of rural Italy, and when he did that, the process of sophistry, how to do things with words in order to clean them up and set them spinning decently once more, found one of its best metaphors. In *E.2.2*, where he discusses various problems of style and language and where, as we have seen (above, p. 2), he finally lays claim to the *aequitas animi* that he searched for in *Epistles 1*, he remarks that one of the functions of the poet who is engaged in writing good (*legitimum*) poetry (it is a sort of lucky by-product of the toil and truth involved in his poetic competition) is, as Mallarmé was to insist and Eliot was to echo, "to purify the language of the tribe," acting toward the words he chooses from like a censor who distinguishes the citizen from the alien (*cum tabullis animum censoris sumet honesti*, 110). As he sorts them out (these, not luminous enough; those, not weighty enough, not dignified enough), he will, among his audacious decisions as to what stays and goes (*audebit*, 111), restore to currency some that have long since disappeared from living speech, decrepit and beyond rejuvenation though they seem (115–18); and, conversely, he will validate new words, ones that ordinary speech (natural speech, perhaps, *parole?*) has invented and brought to the threshold of the lexicon (*adsciscet nova, quae genitor produxerit usus*, 119). Then:

> vehemens et liquidus puroque simillimus amni
> fundet opes Latiumque beabit divite lingua.
> luxuriantia compescet, nimis aspera sano
> levabit cultu, virtute carentia tollet,

ludentis speciem dabit et torquebitur, ut qui
nunc satyrum, nunc agrestum Cyclopa movetur.

(120–25)

Fierce and clear, like nothing so much as a transparent stream,
he will pour out his riches, he will bless Latium with abound-
ing speech. He will trim away what needs trimming, pruning
what's ragged and unkempt, weeding what's worthless—and
all this will seem effortless, yet he will be primed for action, like
one dancing now the satyr, now the Cyclops.

The metaphors here are, in ways that insult neoclassical decorums, not so much mixed as tossed. First (nature) the poet's
parole and the *langue* that supplies it: fierce and pellucid, like a
mountain stream perhaps, that feeds the rivers that make possible the crops of Latium. That pure energy enriches, blesses, the
land. Coming from outside culture, from depths and heights that
civilization is ignorant of (and perhaps dreads), this freedom and
clarity, this powerful, inexhaustible, and transparent purity gives
the indispensible gift.[6] That is the poet in one of his most essential aspects (*vehemens, liquidus;* powerful, pure). But when the
growth begins, when irrigation has done its work, when the
blessed abundance, gift of rich language (*divite lingua*), covers the
Latian fields, then comes, after nature, culture: in the form of
poetic artifice. In another of his aspects the poet trims away all
needless extravagance (some extravagance it needed sometimes,
as he well knows); he polishes what is not smooth enough *sano
cultu,* "avec un soin sagement mesuré," as François Villeneuve
renders it, exactly, in his Budé translation. He weeds out what is
lacking in vitality (again, too much, too little, the defect of the
virtue, the virtue of the defect). Finally, in a moment of antic hay,
the urbane poet mimes pastoral stock characters, now with a
grace that *seems* casual beyond the dreams of Kleist's mad ballet

---

[6] Rudd, 1989, associates the river with Vergil; for other aspects of Horace's river imagery, see Macleod, 1977, 362.

master, à la Debussy, now with an art refined enough to evoke precisely, in its stylish caricatures, the clumsiness of the Cyclops.

Fundet opes (121) echoes the *defudit fruges* of *E*.1.12 and its Augustan cornucopia. But this richness, the edible, nourishing richness of language, beats that gaudy goddess and her world-historical gifts hands down. Latium is blessed with rich language because, now a censor (sophist), now a river, now a gardener, now a mime who changes masks, he selects and eliminates and dedicates, because he chooses, cares for, cherishes *words*. Language, then, is both natural and cultural. We are born with it in us, and we are born into it, into its refinements and its inadequacies, into its deaths and its renewals. Much of it, like the weather and the soil, is beyond our control; but some of it (a bit more than honest men believe, a bit less than dishonest men think) we are, if we listen to what the sophists tell us about it, capable of shaping, of using well. Language, here, is a garden, a natural thing, cultivated (it is also an artificial thing) by the sophist, that cheerful skeptic who strains and sweats to get the garden in shape and yet makes that toil look like tripping the light fantastic (the mood of the passage and its conclusion show an Aristippean brio): it is the sophist who makes the garden grow, who makes it grow both luxuriantly (the beautiful, the savage, the uncivilized) and efficiently (the useful, the ordered, the civilized); it is the sophist (gardener) who makes language (and, in a sense, the world) work (since not a little of the world is, humanly speaking, a world of words). (By the end of this century, of course, this last sentence, not to mention this book and its subject, may be irreparably obsolete; the world we live in, for worse or maybe—who knows?—for better, forever or for a while, is a world of machines, one in which most words and the premodernly technological things they evoke are gradually becoming unfamiliar and irrelevant—but that is another issue, another story.) In this sublime passage, nature and culture are not Hegelianized but properly married. It is a marriage that allows for spats, separations, even knockdown and drag out, china-throwing fights—but essentially this marriage (imperfect though

it is) was made in heaven for earthly humans (imperfect, imper-
fectible, though they are). Here the city sophist and the an-
guished human being whom nature (his farm, his garden) helped
make nearly whole once more achieve their integration: so he
(the poet who watched or imagined watching this integration)
writes a little poem within a larger poem about the goodness and
vitality of gardens and the goodness and vitality of language.

In the *Ars poetica,* in a more somber passage, it is still usage
(*usus*) that decides what old words are allowed to remain and
what new words—after their trial period out in the streets, in the
marketplace and the courtroom, and inside, and in the kitchens
and bedrooms—are permitted to join with older survivors in
what, for the time being, seems to amount to permanence. It has
always been and always will be within our power to coin new
words with the current date (*licuit semperque licebit / signatum
praesente nota producere nomen,* 58–59), but the artifice of this
technic (this aspect of our technology, of our culture) exists
always in the framework set by nature: *ut silvae foliis pronos
mutantur in annos, / prima cadunt, ita verborum vetus interit aetas, / et
iuvenum ritu florent modo nata vigentque,* "Like leaves on the trees in
the forest as the swift years come and go, and the first to leaf is
the first to fall, so, among words, the old ones drop away and the
new ones, in the manner of the youthful human male, flower and
thrive," 60–62. *debemur morti nos nostraque,* "We and all we make
and say and are we owe to death," 63. Then, having recalled
briefly three of the engineering triumphs, of nature (temporarily)
tamed, that Julius and his adoptive son had sponsered (63–68), he
repeats his grim reminder of flux and of mortality: *mortalia facta
peribunt,* "All mortal achievement will be dissolved away," 68.
The imperial (and technocratic) grandeurs in this pattern become
a sort of interlude, a divertissement, a throw-away parenthesis,
bracketed off as they are by the emphatic, divided (and repeated)
memento mori that is the center of this discussion of the decorums of poetic diction. What is begun with the imagery of the
generations of leaves, with its solemn and concise echo of a
genuine, of a Homeric, grandeur (*Iliad* 6.146–49) is resumed and

then ended once the splendors of technology and their demise have been mentioned and dismissed: *nedum sermonum stet honos et gratia vivax*, "Still less will the beauty/honor and use/charm of careful speech [style] show itself long-lasting," 69. Styles, like what the hand fashions from matter, perish. But language, like nature, does not die, and the Homeric celebrations of renewal are again recalled: *multa renascentur quae iam cecidere, cadentque / quae nunc sunt in honore vocabula, si volet usus / quae penes arbitirum est et ius et norma loquendi*, "Many words will be reborn which have now disappeared and many will fall which are now in vogue—all this is up to the discretion of usage, which is the umpire and judge and jury and standard of speech," 70–72. The rhetorical contrast here is, of course, unfair. If ephemeral styles are like leaves and language like the enduring tree that produces them, then balance demands that the triumphs of engineering would stand in the same or a similar relationship with the technology itself, which also endures and which is no less essential to human life than language. But the antagonism between these two rival essences and their proponents is a very old one, and one should not expect an ancient poet—not even this one—to accomplish what modern poets, with their greater experience of technology at its zenith (or perhaps, one hopes, at the beginning of its zenith) have not yet been able to do, that is, to write poems (of the sort that Hart Crane hoped to write) in which poetry and technology could find their union and their equilibrium.

Here again language is natural, yet it is nevertheless simultaneously cultural, for it is subject to *usus,* to the needs and wants that humans have in their interactions and their communal tasks. Language is as elemental as food and drink, sleep and sex, birth and death, yet, like them, language needs culture to become itself most truly; like them, language is, as a specifically human good, something both nature and culture have jointly produced and continue jointly to produce. But in this passage the Homeric and Herodotean grandeurs and the solemn resignations contrast oddly with the peculiar praise of Augustan technocratic grandeurs, which are praised, to be sure, but are dismissed with a faint praise that finally gathers them (with all things human) into oblivion. The monuments of a culture which are specifically technocratic (monuments have some kinship with the frivolous technological caprices that the *Odes* like to torment) will not last as long (despite the ironic *nedum*) as the verbal monuments that seem so much more fragile than they (recall, in this regard, how Ovid will take up this characteristic Horatian warning to imperial appetite for eternity at the close of the *Metamorphoses*). Once these feats of engineering have been dismissed as being relatively ephemeral (in the Ozymandian mode), the dialectical harmony between nature and culture, the garden's balance of life and art (the green world and the sophist's choices), is reasserted—*sub specie aeternitatis,* or under the sign of the Tao. Everything that now exists (one might say, the configuration the 10,000 things now have) will disappear (into something else, as Lucretius, echoing Epicurus, says). But in this moment of time (or eternity, if the truths of *res naturae,* or of the 10,000 things, are understood), our moment in time, it is by means of language that we human beings live most richly the aspects of our lives that are most purely, that is, humanly, ours. We also live by means of our machines, and we could not, apparently, live without them (nor is it likely that we would really want to live without them, since making machines is also part of being human, and, in a sense, machines themselves exist by means of language, and, in a sense, machines themselves are part of our language); but our machines, the machines of the hive, are essentially defined by necessity, and only in an ancillary way do they contribute to the richness of our lives, to our loves and our freedom and our instincts for justice and for compassion, our desire to "minimize the suffering." We need machines (and hives and even emperors) in order to live our lives; but we need language to live our lives in ways that please us, in ways that let us make sense of our lives, in ways that make us feel that our lives are, have been, worth living. That is the poetic way of looking at it, and it is one-sided; but this is, after all, a poem, and Horace is talking about, or rather, making musical images of, the power and goodness of language.

In the *Epistle to Augustus* (2.1.126), Horace ironically begins his list of ways in which the poet is crucial to the state by saying *os tenerum pueri balbumque poeta figurat,* "The poet shapes the tender stammering mouth of the child," meaning that good (successful, civic-minded, patriarchal) poets end up in the *Norton Anthology,* a witticism he had already perpetrated in *C.*2.20 (the deathless bird bard poem). Even deprived of its particular tang here, the truth would remain: poets do in fact (in their fictions, maybe as a mere by-product of their fictions) perform a sophistic function, namely, they teach people what words are and mean (often by reminding them what words aren't and don't mean). When Eliot quoted Mallarmé's "poets purifying the language of the tribe" remark, did he mean what Prodicus or Socrates or Horace means when he claims this function (or what Diogenes means when he says, "I come to deface the coinage")?

Horace as sophist-poet wants to show us (teach is not the word for it—nor, for that matter, is show, but it will have to do) how to clean up the language of our particular tribe for ourselves and for our own purposes.[7] The mode here is a dry and impartial skepticism, and the aim here is freedom. Horace had tried to find freedom in all the wrong places: specifically, he had tried to find it in the hive where his father, and not his father alone, had assumed it to be in its best and surest shape; he had also tried to find it in the wilderness, where it had to be if the hive didn't have it to give; he had tried to find it in his art, and he had in fact found it there in an authentic yet very special and limited, very strange and very seductive, form, but he could not learn the knack of confusing art with life, and he therefore found that even this most vivid, most satisfying freedom was not, finally, enough. Philosophers of various stripes kept muttering—he may have unscrolled and scrolled those volumes dutifully, for a time—that freedom was within, the republic of the heart and all that jazz, but to accept that freedom you have to submit yourself to the bondage of the dogma that proffered the freedom (and you had

[7] See Hirt, 186–97.

to read and even to *memorize* that dreadful prose—so hard on the nerves and not undangerous to one's style); so that was that.

As the years went by and memory and desire began to fashion their usual fragile truce, he stopped trying to make his farm into the desolation he had entered into when he revisited Lebedus in his imagination, and he stopped fearing and hating the city, which doesn't mean that he learned to relove it and to return to it permanently. Pierre Grimal, who has seen the apparent ruins of a possible Sabine farmhouse through the eyes of Flaubert, offers us a Horace's house in the country that has the understated elegance of a fashionable urban pied-à-terre: which would mean that the city and the countryside were each present there, were each fused with the other in that blessed spot near Tibur.[8] Urban rusticity? Rustic urbanity? Who knows where really to place the emphasis or the accent, which is the real (not the apparent) noun, which the adjective (*discors, concors*), when the oxymoronist is Horace? Grimal's, in any case, is a pleasant fantasy; it has a nice ring to it; it certainly suits the dynamics of the antinomies in question. The citified sophist stuck out in the country on purpose, plucking herbs and collecting eggs and overseeing repairs to the dairy or to the slaughterhouse; went for long strolls in the real wilderness (not the tamed one on his extensive grounds) while thinking of new meanings for *virtus* and *ego* and *nos,* for *libertas* and *recte* and *aequus* and *natura,* while sharpening his arguments for putting some of their old definitions in small print at the bottom of the lexicon's page along with other archaisms (never just throw them out or exile them to a rather losable volume "of their own"); went back to the house to get ready for a visit from Fuscus or Torquatus or to write a half a dozen verses for the *Ars,* maybe one (or none) of which will still be a candidate for publication after the month or the year or the life is out.

It's a lazy and very busy, a capricious and a disciplined, sort of life. It's a little crazy, and he is utterly at home in it, utterly committed to it, utterly bound by it. Yet he is almost free within

[8] Grimal, 162–64.

it. He knows now that he will never know the meaning of life or find the words behind the words which will reveal the cosmos as it is to the human mind. The garden has taught him to be patient but not resigned about the poverty of language, about the corruptions and corruptings of societies, about his own inexhaustible, irremediable (but, some of them, somewhat meliorable) failings. It has taught him to give up delusions but not hope; to be ready, in fact, to give up everything (almost—even books? wine? today's lunch?) except the *desire* to be free. And otherwise not to expect miracles, not to spend his time carping at the world (even that part of it which is known as Augustus). Rather, to take zestfully and with a grateful hand what comes; and, of course, to lose his temper only when he has a common cold.

But we are too used to the famous *pituita molesta.*[9] It has been quoted too much, and we feel too comfortable with it. The original *frisson* is not available to us. How to recover the pin that pricks these transcendental hankerings? Horace's head cold deflates the Stoical snake oil synecdochically: all the panaceas are more than suspect. A modern quip less at Vergil than at moderns who misquote him unawares provides an interesting analogue to the Horatian Shanghai gesture. It is the incomparable Mae West: "Love conquers all things except poverty and toothache." That's the spirit of the original.

[9] Préaux, 44–45, argues for *pituita* as "les maux d'estomac," but Cicero's *sapiens si algebis, tremes (De or.* 2.285) should not be ignored here.

BIBLIOGRAPHY

Abrams, M. H. (1971). *Naktural Supernaturalism: Tradition and Revolution in Romantic Literature.* New York: W. W. Norton.

Allen, Walter (with the Horace Seminar) (1970). "The Addressees in Horace's First Book of *Epistles.*" *Studies in Philology* 67: 255–66.

Allen, Walter, et al. (1972). "Horace's First Book of *Epistles* as Letters." *Classical Journal* 69: 119–33.

Anderson, W. S. (1974). "Autobiography and Art in Horace." In *Perspectives on Roman Poetry,* edited by K. Galinsky, 33–56. Austin: University of Texas Press.

Anthony, Heinz (1976). *Humor in der augusteischen Dichtung.* Hildesheim: H. A. Gerstenberg.

Armstrong, David (1989). *Horace.* New Haven: Yale University Press.

Asmis, Elizabeth (1990). "Seneca's *On the Happy Life* and Stoic Individualism." In *Apeiron,* edited by M. Nussbaum, 23:219–55.

Baudelaire, Charles (1964). *The Painter of Modern Life and Other Essays.* Translated and edited by J. Mayne. London: Phaidon. Reprint. New York: De Capo Press, 1986.

Baudrillard, Jean (1988). *Selected Writings.* Edited by Mark Poster. Stanford: Stanford University Press.

—— (1990). *Revenge of the Crystal: Selected Writings on the Modern Object and Its Destiny, 1968–1983.* Translated by P. Foss and J. Pefanis. London and Concord, Mass.: Pluto Press.

Becker, Carl (1963). *Das Spätwerk des Horaz.* Göttingen: Vanderhöck and Ruprecht.

Bernstein, Michael André (1987). "O Totiens Servus: Saturnalia and

Servitude in Augustan Rome." In *Politics and Poetic Value,* edited by R. von Hallberg. *Critical Inquiry* 13.3: 450–74.

Breguet, Esther (1956). "Horace, un homme libre." In *Hommages à M. Niedermann,* 82–89. Collection Latomus 23. Brussels.

—— (1962). "Le thèse *alius . . . ego* chez les poètes latins." *Revue des études latines* 40: 128–36.

Chambers, Iain (1901). *Border Dialogues: Journeys in Postmodernism.* London and New York: Routledge.

Clarke, M. L. (1972). "Horace, *Epistle* 1.13." *Classical Review* 22: 157–59.

Courbaud, Edmond (1914). *Horace: Sa vie et sa pensée a l'époque des épîtres.* Paris: Hachette.

Davis, Gregson (1991). *Polyhymnia: The Rhetoric of Horatian Lyric Discourse.* Berkeley: University of California Press.

Dilke, O. A. W. (1981). "The Interpretation of Horace's *Epistles.*" *Aufstieg und Niedergang der römischen Welt* 2. 31.3: 1837–65.

Dowling, William C. (1991). *The Epistolary Moment: The Poetics of the Eighteenth-Century Verse Epistle.* Princeton: Princeton University Press.

Fabre, Georges (1981). *Libertus: Recherches sur les rapports patron-affranchi à la fin de la république romaine.* Collection de l'école française de Rome 50. Rome.

Foulkes, A. P. (1983). *Literature and Propaganda.* New Accents series, edited by Terence Hawkes. London and New York: Methuen.

Fraenkel, Eduard (1957). *Horace.* Oxford: Oxford University Press.

Frischer, Bernard (1991). *Shifting Paradigms: New Approaches to Horace's Ars Poetica.* Atlanta: Scholars Press.

Gagliardi, Donato (1986). *Studi su Orazio.* Palermo: G. P. Palumbo.

Gamberini, Federico (1983). *Stylistic Theory and Practice in the Younger Pliny.* Hildesheim: Olms-Weidmann.

Gill, Christopher (1988). "Personhood and Personality: The Four-Persona Theory in Cicero, *De Officiis* I." In *Oxford Studies in Ancient Philosophy,* edited by J. Annas, 4:169–99.

Graham, A. C. (1981). *Chuang-Tzu: The Inner Chapters.* London: Unwin.

Grimal, Pierre (1979). *Italie retrouvée.* Paris: Presses Universitaires de France.

Gusdorf, Georges (1991). *Les écritures du moi.* Paris: Odile Jacob.

Harvey, A. D. (1988). *Literature into History.* New York: St. Martin's.

Highet, Gilbert (1974). "*Libertino patre natus.*" *American Journal of Philology* 94:268–81.

Hirschman, Albert O. (1991). *The Rhetoric of Reaction: Perversity, Futility, Jeopardy.* Cambridge, Mass.: Harvard University Press.

Hirt, Hans-Joachim (1985). *Horaz, der Dichter der Briefe: Rus und urbs— die Valenz der Briefform am Beispiel der ersten Epistel an Maecenas.* Hildesheim: Olms-Weidmann.

Holub, Robert C. (1984). *Reception Theory: A Critical Introduction.* London: Routledge.

Immirzi, Elizabeth Glass (1984). "Gardening as a Guide to English Low-Key Practicality." In *Letteratura e seduzione and Discourse Analysis,* edited by T. Kemeny, L. Gueraa, and A. Baldry, 327–34. Atti del VI Congresso Nazionale dell' Associazione Italiana di Anglistica. Fasano: Schena.

Johnson, W. R. (1966). "The Boastful Bird: Notes on Horatian Modesty." *Classical Journal* 62:272–75.

—— (1973). "Propertius and the Emotions of Patriotism." *California Studies in Classical Antiquity* 6:151–80.

—— (1974). Afterword to *Horace: The Art of Poetry,* by Burton Raffel. Albany: SUNY Press. Reprinted in *The Essential Horace,* by Burton Raffel. Berkeley: North Point.

—— (1986). "The Figure of Laertes: Reflections on the Character of Aeneas." In *Vergil at 2000,* edited by John Bernard, 85–105. New York: AMS Press.

—— (1992). "The Death of Pleasure: Literary Critics in Technological Societies." In *The Interpretation of Roman Poetry: Empiricism or Hermeneutics?* edited by K. Galinsky, 200–14. Studien zur klassischen Philologie 67. Frankfurt and New York: Peter Lang.

Kenney, E. J. (1977). "A Question of Taste: Horace, *Epistle* 1.14, 6–9." *Illinois Classical Studies* 2:229–37.

Kerford, G. B. (1981). *The Sophistic Movement.* Cambridge: Cambridge University Press.

Kilpatrick, Ross (1986). *The Poetry of Friendship: Horace, Epistles 1.* Edmonton: University of Alberta Press.

Kindstrand, Jan (1976). *Bion of Borysthenes: A Collection of Fragments with Commentary.* Studia Graeca 11, Acta Universitatis Upsaliensis. Uppsala.

Krupnick, Mark (1986). *Trilling and the Fate of Cultural Criticism.* Evanston: Northwestern University Press.

Kugler, Paul K. (1989). "Jacques Lacan: Postmodern Depth Psychology and the Birth of the Self-Reflexive Subject." In Young-Eisendrath and Hall, 173–84.

Lilja, Saara (1983). *Homosexuality in Republican and Augustan Rome.*

Commentations humanarum litterarum 74. Helsinki: The Finnish Society of Sciences and Letters.

Little, Douglas (1982). "Politics in Augustan Poetry." *Aufstieg und Niedergang der römischen Welt* 2.30.1: 254–370.

Loevinger, Jane (1987). "The Concept of Self or Ego." In Young-Eisendrath and Hall, 88–94.

Long, A. A., and D. N. Sedley (1987). *The Hellenistic Philosophers.* 2 vols. Cambridge: Cambridge University Press.

Lopez, Barry (1989). *Arctic Dreams.* Reprint. New York: Bantam. New York: Macmillan, 1986.

Lovekin, David (1991). *Technique, Discourse, and Consciousness: An Introduction to the Philosophy of Jacques Ellul.* Bethlehem: Lehigh University Press.

Lowe, Adolph (1988). *Has Freedom a Future?* New York: Praeger.

McGann, M. J. (1969). *Studies in Horace's First Book of Epistles.* Collection Latomus 100. Brussels.

Macherey, Pierre (1978). *A Theory of Literary Production.* Translated by Geoffrey Wall. London and New York: Routledge and Kegan Paul. Originally published as *Pour une théorie de la production littéraire française* (Paris: Mospero, 1966).

Macleod, Colin (1977). "The Poet, the Critic, and the Moralist: Horace, *Epistle* 1.19." *Classical Quarterly* n.s. 27: 359–76.

—— (1979). "The Poet of Ethics: Horace, *Epistles I.*" *Journal of Roman Studies* 69: 16–27.

——, trans. and ed. (1986). *Horace: The Epistles.* Rome: Editioni dell' Ateneo.

Malherbe, Abraham J. (1977). *The Cynic Letters.* Society of Biblical Literature, Sources for Biblical Study 12. Missoula: Scholars Press.

—— (1988). *Ancient Epistolary Theorists.* Society of Biblical Literature, Sources for Biblical Study 19. Atlanta: Scholars Press.

Marx, Leo (1964). *The Machine in the Garden: Technology and the Pastoral Ideal in America.* Oxford: Oxford University Press.

—— (1988). *The Pilot and the Passenger.* New York: Oxford University Press.

Mayer, Roland (1985). "Horace on Good Manners." *Proceedings of the Cambridge Philological Society* 211, n.s. 31: 33–46.

—— (1986). "Horace's *Epistles* I and Philosophy." *American Journal of Philology* 107: 55–73.

Minyard, John Douglas (1985). *Lucretius and the Late Republic: An Essay in Roman Intellectual History.* Mnemosyne 90. Leiden.

Misch, Georg (1950). *A History of Biography in Antiquity.* Translated by E. W. Dickes. London: Routledge and Kegan Paul. Originally published as *Geschichte der Autobiographie: Das Altertum* (Leipzig: Teubner, 1907).

Moles, John (1985). "Cynicism in Horace, *Epistles* I." *Proceedings of the Liverpool Latin Seminar* 5:33–60.

Morford, Mark (1987). "The Stoic Garden." *Journal of Garden History* 7.2: 151–75.

Nicolet, Claude (1980). *The World of the Citizen in Republican Rome.* Translated by C. P. Falla. Berkeley: University of California Press. Originally published as *Le métier de citoyen dans la Rome républicaine.* (Paris: Gallimard, 1976).

Olney, James (1972). *Metaphors of Self: The Meaning of Autobiography.* Princeton: Princeton University Press.

O'Loughlin, Michael (1978). *The Garlands of Repose: The Literary Celebration of Civic and Retired Leisure: The Traditions of Homer and Vergil, Horace and Montaigne.* Chicago: University of Chicago Press.

Ooteghem, Jan van (1946). "Horace et l'indépendance." *Latomus* 5: 185–88.

Patterson, Orlando (1991). *Freedom.* Vol. 1, *Freedom in the Making of Western Culture.* New York: Basic Books.

Pelikan, Jaroslav (1974). *The Christian Tradition: The Spirit of Eastern Christendom (600–1700).* Chicago: University of Chicago Press.

Perret, Jacques (1964). *Horace.* Translated by Bertha Humez. New York: New York University Press. Originally published as *Horace.* (Paris: Hatier, 1959).

Pollet, Katha (1991). "Why We Read: Canon to the Right of Me . . ." *The Nation,* 23 September, 328–32.

Préaux, Jean (1968). *Horace: Epîtres, Livre I.* Paris: Presses Universitaires de France.

Putnam, Michael C. J. (1986). *Artifices of Eternity: Horace's Fourth Book of Odes.* Ithaca: Cornell University Press.

Rabinowitz, Peter J. (1987). *Before Reading: Narrative Conventions and the Politics of Interpretation.* Ithaca: Cornell University Press.

Rankin, H. D. (1983). *Sophists, Socratics, and Cynics.* London: Croom Helm.

Rawson, Elizabeth (1989). "Roman Rulers and the Philosophical Adviser." In *Philosophia Togata,* edited by M. Griffin and J. Barnes, 233–58. Oxford: Oxford University Press.

Reed, T. J. (1984). *Goethe.* New York: Oxford University Press.

Ross, David (1987). *Virgil's Elements: Physics and Poetry in the Georgics.* Princeton: Princeton University Press.

Rostagni, A. (1964). *Suetonius: De poetis.* Turin: Biblioteca di filologia classica.

Rudd, Niall (1966; 2d ed., 1982). *The Satires of Horace*. Berkeley and Los Angeles: University of California Press.

—— (1989). *Horace: Epistles II and the Ars Poetica*. Cambridge: Cambridge University Press.

Ste.-Croix, G. E. M. (1981). *The Class Struggle in the Ancient Greek World from the Archaic Age to the Arab Conquests*. London: Duckworth. Second impression, corrected, 1983.

Santirocco, Matthew (1986). *Unity and Design in Horace's Odes*. Chapel Hill: University of North Carolina Press.

Sarsila, Juhani (1982). *Some Aspects of the Concept of Virtue in Roman Literature until Livy*. Studia philologica 16. Jyvaeskylae: University of Jyvaeskylae.

Shackleton Bailey, D. R. (1982). *Profile of Horace*. Cambridge, Mass.: Harvard University Press.

Shaftesbury, Anthony Ashley Cooper (1737). *Characteristics of Men, Manners, Opinions, Times*. 3 vols. 6th ed. London: J. Purser.

—— (1900). *The Life, Unpublished Letters, and Philosophical Regimen of Anthony, Earl of Shaftesbury*. Edited by Benjamin Rand. New York: Macmillan.

Spence, Donald P. (1989). "Turning Happenings into Meanings: The Central Role of the Self." In Young-Eisendrath and Hall, 131–50.

Stack, Frank (1985). *Pope and Horace: Studies in Imitation*. Cambridge: Cambridge University Press.

Starr, Chester G. (1969). "Horace and Augustus." *American Journal of Philology* 90.1:58–64.

Stemplinger, Eduard (1921). *Horaz im Urteil der Jahrhunderte*. Leipzig: Dieterich'sche Verlagsbuchhandlung.

Stenuit, Bernard (1977). "Les parents d'Horace." *Les études classiques* 48:125–44.

Strodach, George K. (1940). "Horace's Individualism Reconsidered." *Classical Journal* 36.1: 1–19.

Tannen, Deborah (1990). *You Just Don't Understand: Women and Men in Conversation*. New York: Ballantine.

Trilling, Lionel (1972). *Sincerity and Authenticity*. Cambridge, Mass.: Harvard University Press.

White, Geoffrey (1985). *Person, Self, and Experience*. Berkeley: University of California Press.

White, Peter (1978). "*Amicitia* and the Profession of Poetry in Early Imperial Rome." *Journal of Roman Studies* 68:74–92.

—— (1982). "Positions for Poets in Early Imperial Rome." In *Literary and Artistic Patronage in Ancient Rome*, edited by Barbara Gold, 50–66. Austin: University of Texas Press.

—— (forthcoming 1993). *Promised Verse: Poets and Poetry in the Society of Augustan Rome*. Cambridge, Mass.: Harvard University Press.

Williams, Gordon (1968). *Tradition and Originality in Roman Poetry*. Oxford: Oxford University Press.

Woodman, A. J. (1988). *Rhetoric in Classical Historiography: Four Studies*. London: Croom Helm.

Young-Eisendrath, Polly, and James A. Hall. (1987). *The Book of the Self: Person, Pretext, and Process*. New York: New York University Press.

Zanker, Paul (1988). *The Power of Images in the Age of Augustus*. Translated by Alan Shapiro. Jerome Lectures 16. Ann Arbor: University of Michigan Press. Originally published as *Augustus und die Macht der Bilder* (Munich: C. H. Beck, 1987).

Zetzel, James E. G. (1982). "The Poetics of Patronage in the Late First Century B.C." In *Literary and Artistic Patronage in Ancient Rome,* edited by Barbara Gold, 87–102. Austin: University Press of Texas Press.

INDEX

Library of Congress Cataloging-in-Publication Data

Johnson, W. R. (Walter Ralph), 1933–
    Horace and the dialectic of freedom / W. R. Johnson.
        p.   cm. — (Cornell studies in classical philology ; 53. The Townsend
lectures)
    Includes bibliographical references and index.
    ISBN 0-8014-2868-8
    1. Horace. Epistulae.   2. Epistolary poetry, Latin—History and criticism.
3. Political poetry, Latin—History and criticism.   4. Horace—Political and
social views.   5. Liberty in literature.   6. Rome in literature.   7. Dialectic.
I. Title.   II. Series: Cornell studies in classical philology ; 53.   III. Series:
Cornell studies in classical philology. Townsend lectures.
PA6393.E8J64   1993
871'.01—dc20   93-17894